# HOW TO THINK LIKE
# THE WORLD'S GREATEST MASTERS OF M&A

# THE LEADER'S EDGE

# HOW TO THINK LIKE
# THE WORLD'S
# GREATEST
# MASTERS OF M&A

## CURT SCHLEIER

M C G R A W - H I L L

NEW YORK    SAN FRANCISCO    WASHINGTON, D.C.    AUCKLAND    BOGOTÁS
CARACAS    LISBON    LONDON    MADRID    MEXICO CITY    MILAN
MONTREAL    NEW DELHI    SAN JUAN    SINGAPORE
SYDNEY    TOKYO    TORONTO

To Barbara,
who made this book and all else possible

**McGraw-Hill**

A Division of The McGraw-Hill Companies

1 2 3 4 5 6 7 8 9 0   AGM/AGM   0 9 8 7 6 5 4 3 2 1 0

ISBN 0-07-136441-2

*This book was set in Clearface by MM Design 2000, Inc.*
*Printed and bound by Quebecor/Martinsburg.*

This publication is designed to provide accurate and authoritative information in regard to the subject matter covered. It is sold with the understanding that the publisher is not engaged in rendering legal, accounting, or other professional service. If legal advice or other expert assistance is required, the services of a competent professional person should be sought.

> —*From a declaration of principles jointly adopted by a committee of the American Bar Association and a committee of publishers.*

This book is printed on acid-free paper.

McGraw-Hill books are available at special quantity discounts to use as premiums and sales promotions, or for use in corporate training programs. For more information, please write to the Director of Special Sales, Professional Publishing, McGraw-Hill, Two Penn Plaza, New York, NY 10121. Or contact your local bookstore.

# CONTENTS

INTRODUCTION

The Urge to Merge Continues to Surge

vii

CHAPTER ONE

## JOHN CHAMBERS

CISCO SYSTEMS

The Art of the Friendly Acquisition

1

CHAPTER TWO

## L. DENNIS KOZLOWSKI

TYCO INTERNATIONAL

Laissez-Faire Mergers

17

CHAPTER THREE

## SANFORD I. WEILL

CITIGROUP

Flying High after All

37

CHAPTER FOUR

## WILLIAM E. SIMON, JR.

WILLIAM E. SIMON & SONS

A Prosecutor in the House

53

CHAPTER FIVE

## HENRY KRAVIS

KOHLBERG KRAVIS ROBERTS & CO.

Making New Managers Accountable—and Partners

69

CHAPTER SIX

# CHARLES WANG
### COMPUTER ASSOCIATES
My Way or the Highway
87


CHAPTER SEVEN

# SUMNER REDSTONE
### VIACOM/CBS
The One Tough Cookie School of Mergers
107


CHAPTER EIGHT

# STEVE CASE
### AMERICA ONLINE
Building a Business on the Premise that Technology
Should Be Accessible
127


CHAPTER NINE

# C. MICHAEL ARMSTRONG
### AT&T
Turning a Battleship on a Dime
145


INDEX
161

# INTRODUCTION

## THE URGE TO MERGE CONTINUES TO SURGE

Every day it seems that the business pages of newspapers are filled with announcements of more and bigger mergers. It's become more than a business phenomenon: It's become a feeding frenzy.

**Blame it on the Internet.**

Investors look at hot young tech stocks that are doubling and tripling every few months, turn to managers of the so-called brick-and-mortar industries, and ask:

"Why can't you do that for me?"

For most established companies, it is virtually impossible to generate the kind of growth investors require internally. So, increasingly, management is turning to acquisitions to fuel the higher numbers Wall Street demands—sometimes whether the mergers make sense or not.

**Blame it on globalization.**

As markets grow, management increasingly feels that it has to have a local presence over there. So American companies are buying European and Asian companies—and vice versa.

**Blame it on the need to dominate.**

Many companies believe they need to be the dominant business in their industry and plan to merge or acquire their way to the top.

None of this is necessarily bad. In fact, some might even say it is the American way.

**There is one question, however.**

If all these top managers are so smart—if their reasoning is so brilliant—why do most mergers end in failure? George Prouty, who is the partner in charge of integration services at KPMG, figures that 70 percent of all mergers are doomed to fail, and he believes that 70 percent of those will fail because of problems integrating the two companies.

Another study by KPMG found that only 17 percent of mergers actually added value to the combined companies, 30 percent produced no discernible difference, and *53 percent actually destroyed value*. As KPMG noted in boldface in its report: **"In other words, 83 percent of mergers were unsuccessful in producing any business benefits as regards shareholder value."**

One of the classic examples of value destroyed is AT&T's ill-fated $7.5 billion takeover of then-computer giant NCR in 1991. NCR lost billions of additional dollars before AT&T finally unloaded it five years later.

And there doesn't seem to be a relationship between the price paid for a company and the likelihood that a merger will succeed. A study by Booz Allen & Hamilton concludes that it doesn't make a lot of sense to obsess over the price that's paid for a company—to worry about whether the deal is too expensive or too cheap. Although that advice at first may appear to be counterintuitive, John Harbison, a Booz Allen vice president and one of those who conducted the study said:

> We're not saying that price doesn't matter, but rather that the price premium needs to be linked to the value that's created....There are deals with significant premiums where value is created and deals with little premium where value isn't created. What this is saying is that if you're an analyst and you see a company pay a high price premium, don't go running to the "sell" button. And if you see a good price, don't run for the "buy" button.

There were, of course, dissenting opinions even before the study—which examined 117 large mergers and acquisitions (M&As) between 1994 and 1996—was released. Mark Sirower, a professor at NYU's Stern School of Business who has written extensively about M&As, was quoted in *The Wall Street Journal* as saying that his research indicated that the larger the premium a company paid, the worse was the shareholder return.

At other schools, the latest fad is evaluating the proper price to pay for a company, based on something called *Real Option Evaluation* (ROV). This is a complicated process that uses complex models developed in part by Nobel prize-winning economists to weigh probability and value in all possible contingencies over the lifetime of a venture. But ROV, too, has been criticized as too gimmicky, too time consuming, and not placing sufficient emphasis on common sense and leadership.

In short, there often really is no logic to M&As. If there were, we'd all be working for the One Corp: the ultimate company and the final product of the world's greatest merger.

The bottom line is that when it comes to M&As, some work and some don't. Consider Boston Scientific's purchase of Sci Med Life Systems. According to Booze Allen, that was the best merger in the two years encompassed by its study. For a premium of approximately $156 million, the merger created a value of nearly $8.2 billion. Not bad! The Boston Scientific management clearly comprises M&A geniuses. Except...

Except that on its very next deal, this very same team stumbled badly when it paid $1.1 billion for a company that had only $95 million in annual sales.

By any measurement, the people profiled on the pages that follow are the Michael Jordans of M&As. Certainly they've all stumbled at times, but their M&A average is higher than Michael's free-throw percentage—which ain't bad.

The following nine people are profiled here:

John Chambers of Cisco;

L. Dennis Kozlowski of Tyco International;

Sanford Weill of Citigroup;

William Simon, Jr., of William E. Simon & Sons;

Henry Kravis of KKR;

Charles Wang of Computer Associates;

Sumner Redstone of Viacom;

Steve Case of AOL;

Michael Armstrong of AT&T.

What do these people have in common? Very little. Some came from wealthy backgrounds and attended the finest schools. Others were impoverished growing up and scraped by. Some got good grades and some didn't. Some were athletic and some were dweebs.

In fact, the only things they seem to have in common are vision and courage. Their vision may vary, depending on the business they're in, but they are somehow able to look into the future, find a place for their companies there, know how to get there, and have the courage to follow that vision. Sometimes an acquisition is a function of broadening a product line: It may be less expensive (in terms of time as well as money) to purchase a company and its product line than to create those products from scratch. Or combining companies in two disparate industries may allow for synergies that would be impossible separately—cross-selling and cross-marketing products, for example.

All of the people listed exude a confidence that comes with being right far more often than they are wrong. And they're also all wealthy, another by-product of being right more often than wrong.

The interesting thing for me is that in investigating their backgrounds, in researching and meeting them, I always walked away with insights that hadn't occurred to me before in the 35 years I've written about business. Sometimes it was just a small nugget—a little kernel, one of those "Gee I never thought of it that way" facts you hit on every once in a while. But more often, I'd walk away with my entire thought process rearranged; the way I looked at other companies would be changed.

I hope you will enjoy that same experience.

CURT SCHLEIER
New York City

# CHAPTER ONE

# JOHN CHAMBERS

CEO and Chairman

CISCO SYSTEMS

# The Art of the Friendly Acquisition

*They've got to see a future. They've got to see a culture they want to be a part of. They have to see an opportunity to really do what they were doing before—or even more. That's what many people fail to grasp. Is your point [that] you're only acquiring the employees? At the rate you're paying for them, you better not be simply acquiring the current market share of the current products. Or you're in deep trouble.*

—JOHN CHAMBERS

Pick up the business section of a newspaper or a business magazine, and the odds are better than good that John Chambers is mentioned somewhere—almost invariably in terms so laudatory, it borders on adoration. The CEO and president of Cisco Systems has delivered another quarter of record profits. Or, perhaps, he's purchased another company—or two or three.

*Worth* magazine named him the top CEO in the country. Technically, the story is about the top *50* executives, but Chambers is the cover boy, numero uno—up from number two the year before. Weeks later, it's *Fortune* magazine's turn. There he is compared to Jack Welch and Louis Gerstner. Chambers is called the business equivalent of Ken Griffey, Jr., and the world is assured that the two are marching in lockstep toward their respective halls of fame.

For the record, this worship of Chambers is not only understandable, but deserved. The statistics are staggering. When he became the company's CEO in 1995, Cisco had a market cap of $9 billion; today, depending upon the temperature of the Nasdaq on any particular day, it's over 50 times that. One share of Cisco bought at $18 when the company went public in 1990 was worth $14,000 after eight splits. With that kind of track record, who wouldn't deify him?

Certainly, there's an element of good fortune in Chambers's success. He was in the right place at the right time. Cisco's primary business is routers—computers on steroids that zip information around the Internet. And as the bandwidth and the number of people who surf grow, so does Cisco's business—at least in theory.

The fact is that the world of the World Wide Web is changing so rapidly that it's only the most astute bosses who are able to keep their companies at the forefront of technology. For Chambers, the key has been a strategy that is based in part on high levels of customer service, well-thought-out acquisitions, and, perhaps most important, a well-conceived plan to thoroughly integrate newly purchased companies into Cisco to ensure that the acquisitions actually work.

Silicon Valley is a far cry from where Chambers was raised, in Charleston, West Virginia. In Charleston, one still sees the shells of the old economy—chemical and other plants long closed—which explains why so many of the city's young people leave. West Virginia may have a lot of country roads, but lately they've all been one way—toward greener pastures elsewhere.

# EARLY INFLUENCES

While it would be melodramatic to say that Chambers came from a family of coal miners, that his career choice was limited to the mines or country and western music, that was hardly the case. Both his parents were physicians, one grandfather ran a bank, and the other managed a construction company. The family was especially close, and Chambers and his two sisters were provided old-school values growing up: Work hard, stay focused, and you'll be successful.

Two stories of that time are revealing:

One, Chambers was mildly dyslexic. As a result, he had difficulty reading and needed to be tutored for two years and work especially hard to catch up. "I got laughed at for being a slow learner," he told *Business Week*. Today, he has a bachelor's and a law degree from West Virginia University and an MBA from Indiana.

Two, Chambers was a young boy fishing with his father in a river moving particularly quickly that day. He lost his footing, slipped, and began to go under. "My dad saw me and started running after me," he told *Fortune* magazine. "'Don't drop the pole,' he yelled. I hung on and he pulled me out. Only later did I understand that he wanted me to concentrate on holding the pole so I wouldn't panic. I trusted him and I survived."

His first job out of Indiana was in sales at IBM. At first he didn't want to take it, believing the job was beneath him. He hadn't gone to school for as long as he did to become a salesman. He'd wanted to go into business for himself. But the recruiter was persuasive, telling him he'd be selling dreams, not technology.

He signed up in 1976 and did well. Ultimately, however, IBM's bureaucracy got to him. During a review, a supervisor once told him that the best way to get ahead was to announce 3 goals and deliver them. Chambers's mistake was that he announced 10 goals, but delivered only 9. Still, there were positive experiences, too: Chambers liked the camaraderie among IBMers, he enjoyed the competitive focus very much, and he also liked the company "uniform." To this day, he almost always wears a suit and tie.

From there, he went to Wang Labs, where he stayed for eight years (1983 to 1991), seeing the company rise meteorically to threaten IBM and then flame out equally rapidly. He had been in charge of sales in Asia and was brought to the United States to help dismantle the once high-flying company. He had to lay off about 5,000 Wang employees, an experience that stays with him to this day. Cisco's policy of not laying off personnel from acquired companies had its roots in that experience.

Cisco was founded by Leonard Bosack and Sandy Lerner, husband-and-wife scientists who ran computers at Stanford University, he for the computer sciences department, she for the business school. The computers were unable to communicate with each other or any computer on campus.

The pair came up with a way for computers from different networks to talk to each other. Their routers forwarded packets of information from one to another, and, as importantly, it did so in a kind of computer Esperanto that let any computer on the network—no matter what kind it was—understand what it was receiving. Bosack and Lerner were unaware of the commercial bonanza they had on their hands and probably wouldn't have founded the company if the university hadn't refused them permission to make routers for friends at several high-tech companies in the area.

Angry, they started Cisco in 1984. As is frequently the case in high-technology start-ups, the founders were better equipped to create technology than manage the company their technology creates. So when Chambers came aboard seven years later, Bosack and Lerner were already gone. But there was no corporate disarray: They left a profitable public company, in large measure because of the efforts of CEO John Morgridge, who had been put in place over their protests.

It was Morgridge who hired Chambers as his number two and heir apparent. Ironically, in hindsight, the Cisco board was unconvinced that Chambers was the right man for the job. The board felt that his background was too sales oriented for him to run a technical company. Morgridge, however, was convinced that Chambers's sales and customer orientation were exactly what the company lacked, and he gave his protege numerous opportunities to make presentations before the board and win the directors' confidence.

# RATIONALE FOR ACQUISITIONS

On one occasion, in 1993, Chambers showed the board that while he wasn't a technology maven, he knew at least enough about the high-tech world to appreciate how quickly things changed in it. He laid out a plan for acquisitions that to this day remains the basis for Cisco's aggressive acquisitions policy.

His position was simple and to the point: With shrinking product cycles, no company can develop everything it needs in-house and still stay on top of its customers' needs. Doing that is too expensive and too time consuming. In many ways, what Chambers proposed flew in the face of conventional Silicon Valley-type wisdom—and bravado—which suggested that if it isn't invented here, it isn't worthy of consideration. Chambers's philosophy was almost diametrically the opposite: We can't possibly invent everything here, so let's be vigilant about opportunities elsewhere.

As *Worth* magazine noted among its accolades to Chambers, he and other Cisco executives "keep an eye on the markets and use their incredibly deep pockets...to buy more companies in whatever direction the industry moves."

Although experience has forced refinements to the plan Chambers presented to his board, the philosophy behind it remains the same: The quest is for customer solutions. Because customers' problems are complex, so is finding the answers.

And, as Chambers told *Business 2.0*, "The companies [that] emerge as industry leaders will be those who understand how to partner, and those who understand how to acquire. Customers today are not just looking for pinpoint products, but end-to-end solutions. A horizontal business model always beats a vertical business model. So you've got to be able to provide that horizontal capability in your product line, either through your own R&D or through acquisitions."

# SUCCESSFUL MERGERS ARE MADE BY HAPPY EMPLOYEES

Being successful, particularly in the area of mergers and acquisitions, is easier said than done. At least part of the explanation for Cisco's success is that Chambers examines companies he's considering buying from a long-range perspective. It's not a question of how much the company will add to the bottom line now or even next quarter or next year—it's a matter of how much it will contribute down the road.

"When we acquire a company, we aren't simply acquiring its current products; we're acquiring the next generation of products through its people," Chambers said. "If you pay between $500,000 and $3 million per employee, and all you're doing is buying the current research and the current market share, you're making a terrible investment. In the average acquisition, 40 percent to 80 percent of the top management and key engineers are gone in two years. By those metrics, most acquisitions fail."

When Cisco acquires a company, it makes a no-layoff pledge. And, in fact, its turnover rate of 2.1 percent for employees acquired through acquisitions is only 10 percent of the industry average. This is no accident: Cisco's ability to retain a company's staff following the purchase of the firm is one of the ways Chambers measures the success of any deal. Therefore, whether Cisco will be able to retain new employees is very much in the center of the process of deciding whether to purchase the business in the first place.

"Employees who have just been acquired can be very uncomfortable," Chambers recognizes. "They have to be made comfortable." How? "They've got to see a future. They've got to see a culture they want to be a part of. They have to see an opportunity to really do what they were doing before—or even more. That's what many people fail to grasp. Is your point [that] you're only acquiring the employees? At the rate you're paying for them, you'd better not be simply acquiring the current market share of the current products. Or you're in deep trouble."

An example of the lengths Cisco goes to to keep its new employees happy was outlined in *The Wall Street Journal*, which followed Cisco's merger with Cerent Corp, a manufacturer of fiber-optics equipment. On the day the merger was announced, a team of Cisco employees handed each Cerent worker a folder that contained basic information about his or her company's new owners, the phone numbers and e-mail addresses of seven top Cisco executives, and an eight-page chart that compared a variety of benefits—vacation, retirement, and medical—at the two companies. Cisco's was frequently better—for example, paying for a new pair of glasses or contacts every year rather than every second year, which had been Cerent's policy.

Over the next two days, Cisco held a series of question-and-answer sessions to reduce the former Cerent employees' uncertainties and allow them to concentrate on their jobs without worrying about the future. And in the first full week after the merger officially took place, Cerent employees had new company I.D.s, business cards, new software already installed on their computers, and even voice mail that was connected to Cisco's system.

It was the smooth attention to detail that made it all work. It wasn't always that way, however. Mimi Cigoux, the woman who headed Cisco's Cerent integration team, learned her job the hard way. A company she used to work for was one of Cisco's early acquisitions, and she saw how her once fast-moving company's progress came to a virtual standstill because its integration with Cisco was not thought through.

# JUDGE A COMPANY BY WHAT IT DID WRONG

That no longer happens. In 1999 one of the gurus on Cisco's merger team told *Fortune* magazine about a couple of ways the company measured potential acquisitions:

"Look for a bad deal. Go over the decisions made. Every start-up should have one glaring mistake it learned from. If the company hasn't done a bad deal, than it's not daring enough. If it's done too many, it's stupid."

The guru also suggested that you can learn a lot about prospects for corporate nuptials by role-playing: "Go over the decisions management made. If you'd make the same ones, the company execs probably think the way you do."

A third factor is speed. Chambers doesn't believe in sweating the small stuff and refuses to nickel-and-dime a potential acquisition to death. "In the Internet economy," he says, "the big won't beat the small; the fast will beat the slow."

However, that doesn't mean the Cisco team is unaware of the small details. Negotiating for one company, a Cisco executive reported an instance in which "the engineering and business teams of a start-up didn't show up at the same time, and each negotiated about how to screw the other guys."

It was a clear sign to pull the plug. It's something Cisco has done—even at the last minute, but not often. The company has its acquisition strategy down to as close to a science as possible, and it starts off in search of firms that share Cisco's vision of the future. As Chambers put it, "If we do it right, we have the chance to become one of the most influential companies in history."

Shared vision is one of five significant criteria Cisco uses to evaluate prospective acquisitions. In addition, it also looks at a company's long-term strategy, the ᴄ... istry between the people of the two companies, and the geographic location of th firm. The last is the easiest to figure out, and Cisco's logic in trying to acquire companies in relatively close geographic proximity to it avoids the potential political headaches typical of multiheaded hydras and poorly thought-out acquisitions, namely, "You'll have the head of finance in one location, the CEO in another, chairman in another, the head of sales in another, head of marketing in another, and you'll actually create the politics forever, in terms of two different cultures. And you never get the efficiencies."

# SHARED VISION

Shared vision is perhaps a bit ephemeral—somewhat difficult to figure out and get a grip on. But it is particularly important, in large measure because of Cisco's no-layoff policy. If the two companies cannot agree on basic philosophical issues (i.e., where the industry is going and what role the newly combined companies should play in the business) *before* the wedding, it does not portend well for the honeymoon and the years thereafter. Instead of working together, they'll be constantly squabbling, creating the kind of tense political atmosphere that is counterproductive to any company, but especially one in the fast-paced high-tech field. Obviously, if a high-tech company loses focus for even a brief period, it can lose market share and its dominance in the field.

Chambers told *Business 2.0,* "We [also] look at a company's long-term strategy and how that fits in with

ours...you've got to have long-term wins for all four con-
stituencies—shareholders, employees, customers and
business partners.

"We also look at similarities in culture and chemistry. The culture and chemistry might be the most
important. It doesn't mean [that] one culture or chemistry is right. But if your cultures are different, they just
never merge together.

"The Bay Networks people would today say I was part
of SynOptics or I was part of Wellfleet [in October 1994
SynOptics and Wellfleet merged to form Bay Networks],
and it lasted forever. You have to avoid the temptation to
say, 'Well, our cultures are different, but I can still make
it work."

Similarly, Chambers feels that the merger between
Compaq and Digital Equipment Corporation was
doomed to fail because the two companies had "different visions. They did not create the short-term wins for
the people of the acquired company. The chemistry and
cultures were night and day in difference, and [there was
no] geographic proximity. Four out of the five elements
we judge acquisitions on, they did not have. People
underestimate how difficult these deals are to do."

That's why Cisco runs away from deals where only
three of the five elements are present and frequently
walks away even when four of five can be verified.

---

## PRACTICE MAKES PERFECT

While Cisco is good at identifying merger prospects, it
is even better at bringing people into the company.
Understandably, the company is most interested in keep-

ing management teams and engineers in place. However, Chambers was deeply affected by laying off 5,000 people during the waning days at Wang, and everyone who chooses can find a home at Cisco. In part because of its successes, in part because employees at acquired companies know they'll be welcomed, the entire merging process has become easier.

Chambers told *Business 2.0* that it's easier now to acquire companies than before, when Cisco was a relatively unknown firm: "We've created a household name. If you're going to be acquired, this is the company to be acquired by." As a result, Chambers or his people frequently get calls from companies his competitors have already made bids on.

The first merger that became the model for future acquisitions involved a company called Crescendo Communications, and it came about because of a Cisco customer, Boeing. Cisco had been negotiating with the airplane manufacturer for a $10 million order, but at the last minute Boeing backed off. It was going to buy a newer technology called "switches" that was simpler and cheaper than, and in some ways superior, to Cisco's routers.

Boeing made it clear that unless Cisco cooperated with Crescendo—that is, unless it created a system that involved both routers *and* switches—it stood to lose the order. This was not the first time Chambers was getting such negative feedback: At about the same time, as David Bunnell notes in *Making the Cisco Connection*, the Ford Motor Company said it was going to shift to switches from routers as well.

Morgridge and Chambers regretted that they'd missed the boat on a previous acquisition possibility a couple of years earlier. So, in 1994, they went to the Cisco board and got permission to acquire Crescendo for $90 million. It eventually cost Cisco $97 million, but the company was a bargain at any price. In two years, Crescendo sales jumped from $10 million to $580 million.

And Cisco was off to the races.

Chambers's oft-stated goal is to become for networking and the Internet what Microsoft is to the software industry—at least, what it was before the antitrust lawsuit. Does anyone doubt him?

# REFERENCES

Bunnell, David, with Brate, Adam. *Making the Cisco Connection: The Story Behind the Real Internet Superpower*. New York: John Wiley & Sons, 2000.

Cringley, Robert X. "The 50 Best CEOs." *Worth*, May 2000.

Daly, James. "John Chambers: The Art of the Deal." *Business 2.0*, October 1999.

Goldblatt, Henry. "The New M&A: Cisco's Secrets. *Fortune*, Nov. 8, 1999.

Greenfield, Karl Taro. "Do You Know Cisco? The Company Whose Routers Rule the Web Now Wants to Be in Your House and on Your Mind." *Time*, Jan. 17, 2000.

Henig, Peter. "Cisco CEO Rocks the House—Again." *Red Herring*, Feb. 17, 1999.

———. "Cisco Is Ready. Are You??" *Red Herring*, Jan. 8, 1999.

Kupfer, Andrew. "Cisco Systems: The Real King of the Internet." *Fortune*, Sept. 7, 1998.

Nakache, Patricia. "Cisco's Recruiting Edge." *Fortune*, Sept. 17, 1997.

Nocera, Joseph, and Faircloth, Anne. "Inside a Hot Stock: Cooking with Cisco." *Fortune*, Dec. 25, 1995.

Reinhard, Andy. "Mr. Internet." *Business Week*, Sept. 13, 1999.

Serwer, Andy. "Two Questions about Cisco. Is John Chambers the Best CEO on Earth? Is it Too Late to Buy His Stock?" *Fortune*, May 15, 2000.

Thurm, Scott. "Joining the Fold: Under Cisco's System, Mergers Usually Work; That Defies the Odds." *The Wall Street Journal*, Mar. 1, 2000.

Tully, Shawn. "How Cisco Mastered the Net." *Fortune*, Aug. 17, 1998.

_____ . "The Newest Member of Tech's Ruling Elite." *Fortune*, Nov. 24, 1997.

# CHAPTER TWO

# L. DENNIS KOZLOWSKI

## CEO and Chairman

### TYCO INTERNATIONAL

## Laissez-Faire Mergers

Tyco looks to newly acquired companies for its new managers and generally finds them right in those companies:

*The existing management is cashing out. They made a lot of money. They're making a lot of money [on the deal]. They no longer have to talk to Wall Street or do the things they used to do to make a living. But somewhere in that organization there are people who are really focused on the product and on the customers. People who've been carrying the ball for a long time.*

*"We find them in diligence, by talking to people in [the acquired company's] organization. We'll get a dozen managers together and listen to their ideas. What would they do differently if they could change something about what happened in the last few years? What would they change?*

—L. DENNIS KOZLOWSKI

**L.** Dennis Kozlowski's first title when he went to work for Tyco International in 1977 was "special assistant for mergers and acquisitions," and his first assignment was to look into what was going on at Dynaco, a company newly acquired by the conglomerate.

Dynaco made stereo speakers, but the word from the consumer electronics show that year was that competitors had achieved technological breakthroughs that threatened to make Dynaco speakers obsolete. Also, Dynaco seemed to be taking inordinately large inventory write-offs.

So Tyco's CEO at the time, Joseph Gaziano, sent Kozlowski to "see if things are really as bad as they seem," Kozlowski recalled. "And he told me to be sure to straighten them out.

"So I went there and sat with management, and it was a mess: nothing but obsolete inventory no one was ever going to buy."

Kozlowski called his boss from the company plane to report his findings. Sitting in a conference room in Tyco's New York headquarters, Kozlowski still chuckles at the memory.

"I said, 'Joe, things are worse than we thought. The write-offs are going to be more than we thought. And we have all this excess inventory. It's a disaster. What should I do?'

"He said, 'Jump!' and hung up the phone."

That was Kozlowski's second week on the job. Things have gone better for him since then. He was named Tyco CEO in 1992 and, over the last eight years, has made more than 100 acquisitions. He's expanded corporate revenues from $3 billion to more than $22 billion and increased the company's market value from $1.8 billion to about $84 billion—not bad for someone who grew up wanting to be a cop like his dad.

Kozlowski was born in Newark, New Jersey. His father was a minor league baseball player—he made it as far as a Triple A team with the New York Yankees' organization—who became a detective with the Newark Police Department. The younger Kozlowski attended Seton Hall University, where he majored in finance and accounting, but had no clear career path in mind: "Some days I wanted to be a state trooper. Some days I wanted to be an airline pilot."

He'd learned to fly as part of his ROTC training in college—he pilots both helicopters and airplanes to this day—and at first tried to get a job selling private aircraft. He was turned down, he says, a smile on his face. "They told me I didn't have any sales background.

"I was literally walking up and down the streets of New York with my résumé, reading *The New York Times* and trying to find a job."

He interviewed at several firms. "It was a good time to be looking," he recalled. "I got a half-dozen job offers. I went with SCM because they offered me $8,400 a year—

which was $200 more than anybody else. So I took the job. It wasn't some grand strategic plan."

SCM Corporation, the old Smith-Corona typewriter company, had developed a dry photocopy process and was making a lot of money at it, Kozlowski recalls. Then "they decided they could be successful at virtually anything they did." He'd signed up with the firm as an executive trainee and spent his early months there, taking management courses as part of the company's training program. He studied auditing and finance, as well as mergers and acquisitions, and discovered he really enjoyed the last.

"I liked the fact of putting companies together and making that work," he says. Even with his scant background in M&A, Kozlowski saw that "SCM did it all wrong.

"I was a junior guy—a due diligence kind of person, and I saw management making a lot of mistakes. This was the go-go days of the '70s, and they invested in food companies, in paint companies, totally disparate acquisitions, high technology, the first portable phones.

"And I was watching this unfold in front of me. I saw no synergies, no links between the businesses. They were just investing in the technology or the hot business at the time. They were probably using the model Harold Geneen was using at ITT, where he was picking up a lot of [unrelated] companies. Most of the acquisitions we did failed in a year or two. They weren't managed. They weren't looked after. All the fun was in the getting. It was like a social disease. Really, they had no management teams concentrating on this—no incentive programs or anything in place."

From there he went to Cabot Corporation, a once-staid firm originally in the chemical business. But the CEO had moved the company into high-performance metals—nickel and cobalt, among others—as well as a number of other unrelated areas. Then a new CEO came in and spun off those companies, returning Cabot to its core businesses.

These were not lessons lost on the young Kozlowski. When he joined Tyco in 1977, he landed in an M&A heaven, or so it seemed to him. At one time, Tyco had gone willy-nilly into the merger business. But by the time he'd arrived, the company had shed itself of 60 unrelated businesses, leaving itself to concentrate on its core industries. Since then, with minor variations and through three CEOs, Tyco has lived with a model that has only the bottom line at its center.

It's a model that's been fine-tuned over the years, to the point where it runs like a well-revved sports car. The model has eight key precepts:

- Never be pressured into an acquisition.

- Identify acquisition targets within the four core areas in which Tyco currently does business.

- Have an operating executive identify and spearhead the acquisition and subsequent integration of the firm.

- Limit acquisitions to companies that are number one or two in their field.

- Don't take chances. Avoid high-tech industries where products have short life cycles.

- Do extensive due diligence—that is, check that

the figures and information you are given are
indeed accurate.

- Make job cuts quickly, usually within the first
  month, and then move on.

- Find new leaders for the company, usually
  internally and in the second or third layer of
  management.

## AVOIDING PRESSURE

There is always pressure on any publicly traded company to keep raising revenues and profits, the more the
better. The pressure comes from individual stockholders, of course, but also from Wall Street analysts who
follow the company and from mutual funds that invest
in it. Some CEOs respond to the pressure to meet Wall
Street expectations by merging and acquiring other
businesses, thereby inflating revenues and, hopefully,
profits.

In fact, some CEOs set acquisition goals for themselves, which puts them into a lose–lose situation. They
can look silly setting unrealistic goals, or they can make
unintelligent choices to meet pie-in-the-sky expectations, Kozlowski feels. "You can't set acquisition goals,
because you don't know. You could force yourself into
doing something you shouldn't be doing. I've been on
boards where the CEO would declare that [one] of his
objectives for the year was to do five due diligences and
at least one acquisition. I don't know how you do that.
If no opportunities for due diligence come up, you've
boxed yourself in."

It is a pressure Kozlowski resists, because he knows that, statistically, the majority of mergers do not add value to the company books. "You could argue that doing a merger or an acquisition can drive up the price of a stock," he says. "The truth is it can just as easily drive down the price of a stock.

"The pressure I feel is to be sure we can continue to grow our business, first of all organically—to have growth, and growth on top of that. *Secondly*, to grow via acquisitions, using our free cash flow to do that. If we come to points in time where we have extra cash flow and we don't have a merger prospect, we buy back our stock. The real focus [isn't on acquisitions, but it] is to do the right thing."

Ironically, on several occasions Kozlowski has said that he probably doesn't need to acquire any company to meet Wall Street expectations. "We feel we can grow our top line by double digits over the next few years and the bottom line by 10 percent to 20 percent," he said in the spring of the year 2000.

Why not play safe? Why risk the potentially deleterious effects of a poorly thought-out merger or even a well-thought-out merger that goes sour? "We'll be generating $3.3 billion from operations and we're being paid a lot of money by the shareholders to do something with that. Buying back your own stock is not terribly creative. Anyone can do that. If we go out and pick the right acquisition, we should get a far better return than buying back our own stock—and thus far we've been able to do that."

There is a sense of Kozlowski's competitive spirit in those words, as though it were a giant game. In fact, a number of years ago, he said, "It is sort of like a big chess game. Sorting out the strategy and determining where we could maximize our opportunities is the most enjoyable."

Kozlowski was a high school athlete—the six-foot, three-inch executive played both football and basketball—so his love of sports and competition is nothing new. But his aggressive, I'm-not-going-to-just-sit-back approach is tempered by reality. The Tyco approach is in part about which companies to buy and how to buy them. But it's also about which not to buy and the willingness to step away from a deal, even if a lot of money has been invested already.

## FOUR CORE INDUSTRIES

For one thing, Kozlowski limits his acquisitions to businesses Tyco is already in, in which company executives already have expertise. That is, they know—or at least have a pretty good idea of—what companies are worth buying and how much they're worth.

Tyco International's core businesses are in telecommunications and electronics (about 34 percent of its sales), in which its companies make everything from printed circuit boards to components found in wireless phones; health-care and specialty products (about 25 percent of sales), selling everything from bandages to syringes and needles; fire and security services (also about 25 percent of sales), selling security services, fire and burglar alarms, and sprinkler systems); and flow control products (16 percent of sales), marketing everything from industrial valves to pipes and couplings.

"We look for products to fill lines," he says. In health care, for example, the goal is to provide "more products for their bundle. We may have a gap in, maybe, a urology product. Or there may be something in some product line that a hospital or nursing home would like to have from us.

"In fire protection and security, we're typically looking to fill in geographic areas. We're in hundreds of cities all over the world. But we do have some gaps in North America. We do have some gaps in Europe and Asia where we'd like to buy into fire and security services." He continues with a lengthy list of the kinds of companies he'd consider acquiring. The list is clear, specific, and well thought out.

## IMMEDIATE BENEFITS

Kozlowski insists, too, that every company Tyco purchases immediately add to the corporate bottom line. That, of course, sounds like a kind of executive pie-in-the-sky rhetoric, but he has been remarkably successful in realizing it. His success is a by-product of staying in businesses in which Tyco already has a presence. So Kozlowski knows going into the deal the kind of synergies that can be achieved by combining manufacturing and distributions systems and a lot of overhead and eliminating some facilities and personnel.

But whatever cost savings are involved, they must be provable: "We won't count on hoped-for synergies or revenue enhancements to justify a deal," he told *The Wall Street Journal* in the spring of 1999. "That's what tends to get so many companies in trouble. We have to see immediate increases in earnings based on costs that we know we can take out."

Moreover, the fact that Tyco executives know the company not only helps them figure out the savings Tyco can achieve, but also gives them a realistic picture of how much additional money they need to put into the company—to automate an assembly line, for example.

"It's all part of our presentation to our board of directors: Here's the base price of the company. Here's the cash we're going to need to upgrade manufacturing, clos[e] manufacturing, combin[e] manufacturing [with something else and pay] severance costs if there are [any]. Then and only then do we look at the returns—after we look at not only the base price but everything we add to it."

While Tyco certainly has some high-technology companies in its corporate portfolio, it moves gingerly in this area. Kozlowski prefers to stick with companies in less glamorous businesses.

"You can criticize us because we're not going to buy a big, high-tech company with big multiples. So if somebody has the next switch for fiber optics, and it has one-thousand gigabytes on it and will work faster than anyone else's and wants to sell it at 90 times earnings—or projected earnings—we're not going to be the one buying it. We're not going to take a risk at that level. We're not going to buy into these high-tech, high-risk businesses. We're going to buy into fundamental businesses that we know we're going to get our cost out of right away."

That's not to say the company doesn't make mistakes. In 1992, Tyco purchased a small pipe manufacturer. Tyco was in the business and this company was available, as Kozlowski puts it, "on the cheap. We bought it for around $20 million and put another $60 million or $70 million into it and started making pipe.

"Soon our raw material prices, the steel coming into us, was more expensive than the price the big guys were selling the pipe for on the marketplace. We realized we were in a tough neighborhood. No matter how tough we were, no matter how smart we were, no matter how fast we were, we knew we were not going to be allowed into this business."

Was it a conspiracy? Kozlowski looks upon it as an education: "The lesson we learned is that unless you're number one in the business or a real strong number two, don't mess around with it. Don't even go there. There's no such thing as a cheap acquisition. Think this thing through. And take a hard look at it."

Tyco ended up liquidating the company, selling off the inventory, and garnering a major write-off. "But the lesson there was good. And that was the last one we screwed up."

---

# FINDING POTENTIAL TYCO COMPANIES

There have been over 100 acquisitions since then. "We're constantly on the prowl to make things happen," Kozlowski says. "And part of our culture, our operating people's culture, is to have a list of things that they are looking into.

"We began this process in 1976 when we were a $20 million company. And today we'll do about $28 billion in revenues. It's not like we just started doing this. In 1977 we were a $100 million company; in 1978 we probably were a $300 million company. So now this is part of our culture. We have people who do mergers and acquisitions, who have financial expertise and legal expertise in that.

"Realistically, thousands of our operating employees are deputized to do mergers and acquisitions. It's part of their culture. It's part of what they do. They know how to do diligence. They know how to get returns. They know how to identify operating entities that would become good acquisition candidates for us.

"In so many organizations, headquarters people [start] the acquisition process and give it to an operating division. Here the operating people are signed up to an acquisition from day one. Acquisitions are charged to their P&L from day one. Their bonuses and personal incentive plans become involved right away. The goodwill cost, the amortization, all those things are owned by the operating people, so they're buying into this. This is a real team approach."

Beyond operating personnel, there's someone on the corporate staff whose full time job is to track core businesses and chart the 10 best companies that each of its core businesses might be interested in. "We rank them and show what product lines they would fill. We regularly call the CEOs of these companies and say, 'if you ever want to get together or would you like to get together for breakfast, we'd like to talk to you about why we think our two companies would be a good fit."

Tyco doesn't believe in hostile takeovers. Kozlowski feels that the business of combining the cultures of two different companies is difficult enough without "a group of employees and people in that company who feel [that] somehow you're violating their turf," Kozlowski said a few years ago in an interview on a CNN financial TV show.

It's something he learned from experience in 1981, when he was put in charge of Ludlow, a plastics company Tyco had just taken over in an unfriendly deal. "It turned out to be a terribly difficult experience, because the ill will and rancor of the takeover battle drove many of the good people we wanted and needed out of the company," he told *The Wall Street Journal*. "It took much longer than it should have to put the pieces together again at Ludlow."

As a result, there have been no hostile takeovers during Kozlowski's watch. If the CEO of a certain company isn't interested in pursuing a deal with Tyco, well, there are usually other fish in the sea. Given the trend toward globalization and a worldwide mania for mergers and acquisitions, the CEO may even change his or her mind. That's what happened, according to *The Wall Street Journal*, when Tyco first approached U.S. Surgical Corp. in 1993 about a possible acquisition. CEO Leon Hirsch said no, thank you, at the time, but five years later, with competitors consolidating around him, he changed his mind.

Given the company's reputation, of course, investment bankers come calling all the time. But no matter how or where the idea for an acquisition originates, Kozlowski insists that it have an internal champion committed to its success, to shepherd it through the process.

Because he wants to ensure the success of each acquisition—or at least minimize mistakes—Kozlowski places a great deal of emphasis on due diligence, a fact that may have something to do with being a cop's kid. "I'm focused on really getting to the bottom of things. I probably doubt most things other businesspeople tell me when they're selling me a company. I just came from an environment where you just have to show it to me.

"I don't know if that comes from growing up on the streets or [if it's a function of being] the kind of person the stars make you to be. But as a result, I think I've spent an awful lot of time on diligence and do ask a lot of detailed questions. I'm suspicious by nature. Overall, being suspicious makes us really do our diligence."

Tyco walks away from 9 of 10 potential acquisitions after conducting due diligence, often an expensive stroll, since due diligence can cost as much as $300,000. Kozlowski walks "if the company's growth projections are not going to be met—because that determines our price. And that happens often. If we find something we don't like about the accounting or the bookkeeping. That happens sometimes.

"Or if we stand back and look at the business and decide it's not a sustainable growth business, just a one- or two-year deal and the product will be obsolete. And there are no plans in the pipeline to replace it. Also, there are situations where they're over the line on conservative accounting—where we feel the accounting would not meet our standards, not pass our auditors."

As a final check, Tyco uses both internal and external auditors to vest the due diligence, "to give us a totally objective view.

"One could argue that your own auditors are pleased by acquisitions because that gives them a bigger base to audit from. However, using other auditing firms aside from your own, you could argue that they want to prevent you from having a disaster which you'll hold against them forever. As a result, they'll aggressive[ly] look for what's wrong."

Once a company is acquired, Tyco doesn't attempt to change the company's culture, although it certainly tries to make it leaner. "What we do attempt to influence is if the company is heavily bureaucratic or has a lot of committees, we try to influence that, make that kind of stuff go away. Because here at Tyco we don't have regularly scheduled meetings. We try to communicate on a daily basis without having a lot of vice presidents....

"Because we don't have a lot of group vice presidents here, acquired companies don't get a lot of interference from corporate headquarters. We've found in acquisitions we've done, where we've gone from matrix organizations to the bottom-up kind of organization we have here, it really reduces cycle time for customers and we get new products through cycles at warp speeds compared to what had been done in the past. It makes for much more crisp decision making throughout the business, and people running the businesses feel a lot better about themselves."

# ENTREPRENEURIAL SKILLS VALUED IN KEY EXECUTIVES

Tyco has only about 70 employees at its corporate headquarters. The heads of the four major operating units are posted in the field, near plants and customers.

Independence is important if Tyco is going to attract what Kozlowski calls executives in the "Tyco mold." Asked to describe that mold, he says that the people who fit it are "entrepreneurial with strong entrepreneurial [common] sense or skill sets in business. They are not bureaucratic, but true leaders. They do the right thing and not [just] try to do things right. These are people who would succeed wildly running their own business without a Tyco Corporation."

In a typical situation, top management of the acquired company does not make the Tyco transfer. "That's a foregone conclusion when we do the deal. The existing management is cashing out. They made a lot of money. They're making a lot of money [on the deal]. They no longer have to talk to Wall Street or do the things they used to do to make a living. But somewhere in that organization there are people who are really focused on the product and on the customers—people who've been carrying the ball for a long time.

"We find them [during due] diligence, by talking to people in [the acquired company's] organization. We'll get a dozen managers together and listen to their ideas. What would they do differently if they could change something about what happened in the last few years? What would they change?"

Sometimes it boils down to a gut reaction. "You do your best," Kozlowski says. "Ask a lot of questions. But at the end of the day it comes down to your saying 'I've seen a person like this before, and she's going to work out. Or there's something about their style that leads me to believe that they're too lofty or not in touch with their business or don't know what they're talking about or just turn you off. So you operate on gut or intuition."

Kozlowski told *The Wall Street Journal*, "We typically find our new leaders a layer or two below the top. We look for good operators who have hung in there despite all the frustrations of bureaucracy and matrix management and stayed close to the products and customers. They are often people who have held the company together for years, but have never been recognized for it."

Kozlowski feels that AMP, a Harrisburg, Pennsylvania-based manufacturer of electronic connectors is the best example of how Tyco picks people to run the companies it acquires. AMP was the subject of a hostile bid by Allied Signal. At first, AMP repulsed Tyco's friendly overture, but ultimately the electronics company changed its mind. Robert Ripp, the CEO who had delivered AMP to Tyco, was not to make the transition. Juergen Gromer, AMP's senior vice president of worldwide sales, was named as his replacement.

As Kozlowski recalls, when Gromer was interviewed, he said all the right things:

"He said, 'I'm spending all my time dealing with all the bureaucracies in Harrisburg and London and Japan. Our decision making is virtually at a standstill. It's taking us a year and a half to get new products into the marketplace. We're not supporting our customers. Our focus at the company is internal instead of external. I think AMP should be organized in a classical kind of bottoms-up style. Somebody should be at the helm to do that.'

"Juergen wasn't pitching for himself to have the job, but he just was frustrated by the way the business was organized. After meeting a lot of people in the organization, we decided Juergen had the leadership skills to [accomplish] this. He was well respected at AMP and he was well respected by the customers. So we gave Juergen the job, and allowed him to implement the reorganization he came forward with."

Gromer implemented about $1 billion in cost reductions—layoffs, the closing of dozens of superfluous plants and offices, and centralized procurement. That's the equivalent of approximately 15 percent of AMP's revenues. Gromer's impact was immediate, Kozlowski says.

"A year later AMP's product sales were up 70 percent, [and] our cycle time is [now] down to 3 or 4 months from about 18 months for new products. And we have more than quadrupled our products in the organization."

Once an acquisition is completed, personnel decisions are made relatively quickly—within the first 30 days. "That way, we can tell employees that's all in back of us. Here are the new incentive programs. Our mission is to grow. We'll give you all the tools: everything you need and a lot of independence."

Another key element in the company's success is that it rewards its people extremely generously. No one gets paid anything unless net income grows at least 15 percent—but their remuneration grows quickly once that level is achieved. Kozlowski believes strongly that senior managers have a vested interest in the company's success by being major shareholders in the firm. (Kozlowski claims that 90 percent of his net worth is in Tyco stock.) The bonus program is tied into that philosophy.

Senior managers receive 90 percent of their incentive pay in stock and only 10 percent in cash. Further down the ranks, incentives are split 50–50 between cash and stock. Nearly everyone—and the company currently has 120,000 employees in over 80 countries—shares in the success. The only exception is unionized workers whose contractual restrictions come into play.

Because compensation is tied to the bottom line, there is certainly a temptation to play with the numbers or to make short-term decisions that may not be good in the long term.

Kozlowski concedes, "That's a criticism of a program like this. But we also have long-term incentive programs in place. Probably the best testimony that this works is that over the last seven or eight years, not a single division head or any key person has left for any reason. Part of the culture here is that you're going to be here, you're going to be around, and we're not going to let you cut research and development—we're not going to let you wipe out your sales force. There are checks and balances here. We're really not going to let you do anything short term."

His advice to new employees? "Stay focused on the business. Become the number one in the marketplace. We'll give you the tools, the resources, to get that done. When you screw up and make a mistake, tell me the bad news right away and tell me what your correction plan is. We all make mistakes and things happen. But continue to grow your business."

# REFERENCES

Collis, David J., and Montgomery, Cynthia A. "Creating Corporate Advantage." *Harvard Business Review*, May 1, 1998.

Interview with L. Dennis Kozlowski, May 2000, New York, NY.

Laing, Jonathan R. "Tyco's Titan: How Dennis Kozlowski Is Creating a Lean, Profitable Giant." *The Wall Street Journal*, Apr. 12, 1999.

Lublin, Joann S., and Maremont, Mark. "A CEO with a Motto: Let's Make a Deal." *The Wall Street Journal*, Jan. 28, 1999.

Schwartz, Nelson D., and Creswell, Julie. "Retire Rich." *Fortune*, Aug. 16, 1999.

# CHAPTER THREE

# SANFORD I. WEILL
## CEO
### CITIGROUP

## Flying High after All

When cutbacks in military spending meant he wouldn't become a fighter pilot after all, Sanford I. Weill found another way to soar:

*I always thought I'd like some form of business. I didn't know what kind of business I'd go in[to]. I think life is sort of like a competition, whether it's in sports, or it's achieving in school, or it's achieving good relationships with people. And competition is a little bit of what it's all about.*

—SANFORD I. WEILL

Sanford (Sandy) Weill never intended to go into the world of high finance. He'd set his sights on becoming a high flyer of a different sort—with the United States Air Force.

Weill had finished Air Force ROTC at Cornell University in 1955 and had about six months before he was scheduled to report to Lackland Air Force Base for additional training. In the interim, he was casting about for something to do to support himself and his young bride.

As he recalled for the Academy of Achievement, "In walking around New York and looking for new ideas, one day I happened to walk into a brokerage office, and it seemed exciting."

At about the same time, President Eisenhower was cutting back military expenditures, so it turned out that if Weill was going to do any high flying, it wasn't going to be out of Lackland after all.

Thus, from a combination of chance and coincidence, a career was born.

When Weill made his career choice, Wall Street was so different than it is today, that it almost seems like ancient history. It was still the stock market then, not the stock rocket it has become lately. It was a time when the volume on the exchange was low—a day when a million and a half shares traded generated comments. It was also a day when the obstacles to getting into the business were formidable—unless you had the proper connections. "Unless you were wealthy, you couldn't get into the business," he recalled.

Weill's family, however, wasn't wealthy or part of any in crowd with the right connections. He applied for, and was rejected by, several large brokerage training programs. But that didn't stop him. When that plan didn't work out, Weill figured there was more than one way to make a fortune—and he wasn't afraid to start at the bottom en route to it. His first job was as a runner at Bear Stearns & Company. From there, he moved into the back office.

It appears an unlikely start to a successful career in finance, but it didn't deter Weill. In fact, he's always thrived on adversity, a trait he demonstrated again and again over the course of his career. In a sympathetic profile, *Forbes* magazine described him as a man who "hates losing. When he does lose, he's soon plotting how to recoup on the loss."

That he couldn't get into a training program was less a defeat than an obstacle to be overcome—a source to get his juices flowing.

"When I was a young kid and used to deliver newspapers, I liked the idea of competing and trying to get more new subscriptions than somebody else." he said. "And I always thought I'd like some form of business. I didn't know what kind of business I'd go in[to]. I think life is sort of like a competition, whether it's in sports, or it's achieving in school, or it's achieving good relationships with people. And competition is a little bit of what it's all about."

He honed much more than his competitive spirit as a youngster growing up. He became aware of numerous possibilities. Weill was born in Brooklyn, New York, the son of a moderately successful dress manufacturer, an immigrant from Poland who came to the United States with nothing. Here was a man who saw the potential of America fulfilled.

"I think the American dream says that anything can happen if you work hard enough at it and are persistent and have some ability," he said. "The sky is the limit on what you can build and what can happen to you and your family."

---

## STARTING SMALL AND BUILDING AN EMPIRE, ONE COMPANY AT A TIME

Weill didn't demonstrate his abilities—at least academically—early on. His parents were concerned enough about his grades to enroll him in a military school for a year, hoping the discipline would improve his attitude. It worked: "All of a sudden, I went from not doing well to beginning to do better, and I stayed there for four years. I think that the experience in the military school— where in the beginning you learn how to take the punishment before you dish it out—teaches you a lot about how to get along with people and put yourself in the other person's perspective."

In 1960 Weill and three friends scraped together $200,000 and started a brokerage company, Cogan,

Berlind, Weill & Levitt. The company prospered, and the partners entered the M&A fray in 1970 when they offered to acquire the troubled and much larger brokerage firm Hayden Stone.

Hayden Stone was one of several old-line companies that were having a difficult time adjusting to the new environment on The Street. While the stock market volume was rising in quantum leaps, the traditional and lucrative fixed-commission structure was being deregulated by the Securities and Exchange Commission. Thus, at a time commission levels were going down, the cost of servicing clients—back-office expenses—were rising. It was a chaotic atmosphere that the white-shoe firms that made up the Wall Street establishment were unused to. They had always existed in a genteel, upper-crust, country club kind of circumstance, and many discovered that they were unable to cope with a market invaded by the hoi polloi.

But Weill found the situation seductive for several reasons. For one thing, in the same way that rejection whet his competitive appetite when he was turned down for the brokerage training programs, so did the challenge of making Hayden Stone whole. Rather than turning him away, the potentially high stakes served as a temptation.

"When you say, 'risk is involved,' I think this: If a person is not willing to make a mistake, you're never going to do anything right. Because most of us are not perfect, therefore, I think it's important to learn to be a risk taker, because it's important to be a loser before you can be a winner.

"And learn that when you do make a mistake, you'll surface that mistake so that you can get it corrected, rather than...try and hide it and bury it. [Then] it becomes a much bigger mistake, and maybe a fatal mistake."

---

# LESS COMPETITION WHEN BUYING TROUBLED COMPANIES

While the acquisition of Hayden Stone was risky for Weill and his partners, it was a calculated risk. Weill did not, as one magazine at the time said, "bet the ranch" on the acquisition. He knew exactly what he was doing.

He studied the situation and immediately recognized and, more importantly, understood a basic axiom of M&A, one that would stand him in good stead throughout his career: It's a lot easier to buy a troubled company than a firm that is minting money. Troubled companies are cheaper, of course: There's less competition to become the owner of a dog—and a sick dog at that—so less capital is required to make the purchase.

But, as important, failing companies invariably have supporters who desperately want them to survive and will do most anything to encourage potential suitors: its present owners, who think a fire sale price is better than nothing; banks and other lenders, who have loans outstanding that would be wiped out—or virtually wiped out— in the event of a bankruptcy; or, as in this case, the New York Stock Exchange, which clearly did not want one of its most prominent member firms to go belly up.

Consequently, not only did the Exchange approve what once almost certainly would have been an unlikely deal, but it also provided $6 million to Cogan, Berlind, Weill & Levitt to cover any losses the company might incur.

Weill has consistently proved expert in getting outside help to underwrite a portion of the risk when making a purchase. In 1974, when he bought Shearson, Hamill, Weill arranged for Citibank (ironically) to roll over an outstanding loan it had with Shearson. Just a few years later, Cogan, Berlind, Weill & Levitt bought Loeb Rhoades Hornblower, another firm on the rocks. As part of the deal, Weill got John Loeb, a member of the founding family, to throw a reported $30 million into the pot.

But creative financing has been only a small part of the Weill modus operandi. After all, if he couldn't turn a troubled company around, Weill would be overpaying at any price. Consistently, however, he has shown that he knows exactly what he is doing. "I'm not smarter than anybody else," Weill has said. "I just understood this [the brokerage] business better than anyone else."

No one ever got wealthy *under*estimating Weill's abilities to pull off a deal. In 1991 *Forbes* magazine confidently suggested that Weill had bitten off more than he could chew with his latest acquisition. Just two years later, *Forbes* said "oops" and sang his praises.

In 1997 an economics professor told *American Banker* magazine that one of Weill's acquisitions could not work. Give the professor an "F."

# IT'S NOT JUST VISION; IT'S KNOWING WHERE TO LOOK

Weill did more than understand the basics of the brokerage business. He combined that understanding with vision. While others were mired in the past, Weill was working toward the future. In the 1970s, as Weill was building his empire, most of establishment Wall Street was still focused on institutional investors. Weill, however, foresaw the emergence of the retail customer.

Whereas other firms were concentrating on getting customers, Weill concentrated on the operations end of the companies he bought. He recognized—as they did not—that competitors were failing because their back-office operations were inefficient. They couldn't handle the ever-increasing volume.

Roger Berlind, one of Weill's partners at the time, noted, "In those days, most people thought the back office was for people in green eyeshades. But Sandy was fearful of anything going wrong down there. He became familiar with it."

Weill's logic should have been apparent to everyone. The more efficient the back office is, the more a company can increase sales without increasing staff. Moreover, the more efficient the back office is, the less paper shuffling that goes on.

Unlike many other executives with vision, Weill also reveled in details. If a problem couldn't be resolved at a lower level, employees were encouraged to call the boss and were assured that a response would be forthcoming within 24 hours.

He was also prepared to work harder than anyone else—hands-on, too. One colleague tells a now renowned anecdote of how Weill showed up late one Saturday night in the back office of a firm he had recently acquired dressed in his pajama tops. He'd been home asleep and decided to make sure that the transfer of customer accounts went smoothly.

It almost always did. By 1981, Shearson Loeb Rhoades was the second largest brokerage house in the country—behind only Merrill Lynch—and had a reputation for having the finest, most efficient back-office operation in the business. That's when the company was sold to American Express for $1 billion—that's *billion*.

Weill has at different times offered several reasons for selling out. He said he was bored: "I got a little bit tired doing the same thing, and the world was beginning to change," he told the Academy of Achievement. "We asked ourselves, 'How can we do something different?' And the idea emerged that maybe we should merge with American Express and become part of the corporate establishment. I felt I'd learn a lot of different things doing that."

But he's also noted that brokerage firms were generally undercapitalized and that the idea of partnering with American Express with its deep pockets was, "no question, the least riskiest thing [I'd] ever done."

He was named Amex president in 1983, whereupon he was given one of his most interesting assignments: to turn around the company's troubled Fireman's Fund insurance subsidiary. Weill immediately showed how decisive he could be slashing staff, moving executives around, repricing products, and selling some businesses. He took a single-minded, pragmatic approach, identifying subsidiaries that weren't pulling their own weight and getting rid of them.

Yes, some of them were supposedly there for strategic reasons: A Hong Kong–based joint venture was to be a stepping stone to the entire Pacific rim; another based in London was the stepping-stone to Europe. But the ever practical Weill wouldn't hear of it. As *Forbes* magazine noted, "He's interested in core markets. If a company wasn't central to [Fireman Fund's] U.S. underwriting business and wasn't earning a proper return, it had to go."

Despite his successes, it became clear that the match between Weill and Amex CEO and Chairman James Robinson was not made in business heaven. Weill has attributed his leaving to a culture clash:

"It didn't work out because our entrepreneurial philosophy didn't fit into that kind of culture. We didn't build the kind of company that we could have built together."

Rumors circulated that the business version of the film *The Clash of the Titans* (*Egos*) played regularly at American Express headquarters. Whatever the reason, Weill left Amex with a wad of money. He tried to use it to buy Fireman's Fund, but the American Express board ultimately rejected the bid in favor of taking the company public. (The board reportedly had reservations about selling the company to an insider, leaving themselves open to legal action if the price was perceived as too low or the terms too favorable.)

So Weill suddenly found himself unemployed. He put a positive spin on it:

"There was a period of a year [after leaving American Express] when I didn't do anything. But you know what? I think one of the greatest periods in my life is when I decided to leave American Express, because most people don't really get to know what people think about them when they're alive....

"You always wonder, 'Are people friendly with you— or [are] people paying attention to you,...making believe they like you because of your position and what you can do for them.' And what I think was really great was that when I left, I didn't have this position of power at American Express."

# EVEN MAJOR LEAGUERS STRIKE OUT ONCE IN A WHILE

"And the first thing that was important about [my leaving] was [that] it helped my relationship with my children a lot, because they always looked at me as this person who couldn't do anything wrong and therefore they couldn't contribute [anything to me]. And all of a sudden, they saw their father was vulnerable, and it helped [us] create a more equal kind of relationship with each other, [one] where we respect each other a lot, and that was very important to me. The second thing is that I found out [that] a lot of people liked me for [being] me, and not because I was the president of American Express."

While that's a nice positive spin, the inactivity almost certainly had Weill champing at the bit. Perhaps that's why his next move—a run at BankAmerica—turned out to be one of the few significant blunders in his lengthy career.

One of the lessons Weill says he learned at American Express "was that management skills in one kind of financial service carry over to another." BankAmerica seemed the perfect company for Weill to test that theory. In 1985 the bank had recorded a loss of over $335 million and had eliminated its dividend. Believing he had the support of the BankAmerica board, Weill wrote the company's CEO offering $1 billion in equity to replace him. That was a serious misjudgment: He did not have the backing he anticipated. On the contrary, the outside directors on the board sent him a chilly letter that read, in part, "The outside directors unanimously agreed that they have no interest in considering you as a candidate for the chief executive officer's position." It was a devastating blow. But then Weill's luck changed. A couple of executives at Commercial Credit Corporation, a Baltimore-based and troubled subsidiary of Control Data, read an article in *Fortune* magazine that was headlined "Sanford Weill, 53, Exp'd Mgr, Gd Refs." It seemed he was just what they were looking for. Commercial Credit was a down-and-out consumer finance company that Control Data had on the market for over a year. In fact, it had been offered to Weill when he'd been at American Express. Now they wanted him to take another look. Control Data was in trouble, they said, and that was affecting its Commercial Credit subsidiary.

Weill listened, looked, and liked what he saw. Commercial Credit was a solid if unspectacular company, with a lending business, an insurance company, and other units, a product of its aimless diversification. Much of what was wrong with the company, Weill felt, was easily correctable.

Weill approached Control Data with an offer: Make him CEO, and he'd take the company public. Control Data bought the argument, and eventually Wall Street bought the stock—happy to bet that Weill would have the same success with Commercial Credit that he had with Cogan, Berlind, Weill & Levitt.

Again, Weill moved quickly and decisively. He gathered around him a cadre of executives with whom he had worked previously. His experience at American Express taught him a valuable lesson: "I think what we want[ed] to do is create a collegial kind of environment where our enemy is the competitor and not the person who sits in the next office. All of us are refugees from large organizations with bureaucracies and committee meetings, and we vowed to build an organization that would not have that kind of stuff."

He also took a tack he would take again and again: loading his managers with options and restricted stock they had to take a blood oath not to sell. When Commercial Credit went public, its directors were paid only in stock. "Very few companies did that in those years...part of what our top executives get paid every year is in stock rather than cash. At the time, all 60,000 [Commercial Credit] employees were given stock options."

Clearly, Weill believes that "ownership is really key. Ownership gets people to think like owners, to think that the company is really theirs. Really good ideas, innovative ideas, come from the bottom[s] of organizations—not really the tops of organizations. [The ideas come from a level at which] people are dealing directly with the customers and understand what the market wants rather than dictating what the market wants. [It's a place] where people can see the silly things the chairman may be doing or better ways to do it. We encourage people to think that way. The best way to do that is through ownership."

It wasn't only the top executives who got a piece of the pie: Weill gave each branch manager greater responsibility for the bottom line—and rewarded those who did well with bonuses that amounted to as much as double their salaries. The change in attitude was immediate.

The wife of one manager approached an executive handing out bonus checks and said, "I used to complain when my husband got home at 6:30 and dinner was cold. Now I want to know why he's not working until 8." So much for true love!

It worked. In 1985, the year before Weill purchased the company, Commercial Credit's share of the personal loan market was 3 percent. In 1987, the first full year after Weill took over, the company's share more than doubled, to 7.5 percent. Between 1987 and 1992, the company's earnings grew at a compound rate of 23 percent.

Commercial Credit also became the springboard for a continuing stream of acquisitions: Primerica (including Smith Barney), Travelers, Shearson, Aetna, Salomon Brothers, and then, in 1998, the merger between Travelers and Citicorp to form Citigroup. Originally, Weill and Citicorp head John Reed were co-CEOs, but Reed has retired. And once again, Weill is flying high and solo.

## REFERENCES

Connelly, Julie, and Abelson, Reed. "The Return of Second Hand Rose." *Fortune*, Oct. 24, 1988.

Greenwald, John. "Wall Street's Highflyer." *Time*, Oct. 6, 1997.

Interview of Sanford I. Weill with Academy of Achievement, May 23, 1997.

Kantrow, Yvette D. "Sanford I. Weill: Sculptor of the Future." *American Banker*, Dec. 18, 1997.

Laderman, Jeffrey M. "Sandy's Triumph." *Business Week*, Oct. 6, 1997.

Linden, Dana Wechsler. "Deputy Dog Becomes Top Dog." *Forbes*, Oct. 25, 1993.

Loomis, Carol J. "Citigroup: A Progress Report." *Fortune*, Nov. 23, 1998.

———— . "Citigroup: Scenes from a Merger." *Fortune*, Jan. 11, 1999.

———— . "Traveler's: The Chairman Is Happy." *Fortune*, April 28, 1997.

———— . "Sanford Weill, 53, exp'd mgr, gd refs." *Fortune*, May 12, 1986.

Pouschine, Tatiana, and Greer, Carolyn T. "Be Careful When You Buy From..." *Forbes*, Apr. 15, 1991.

Sachar, Laura. "Sandy Weill's Expansion Team." *Financial World*, Aug. 11, 1987.

Sellers, Patricia. "Behind the Shootout at Citigroup." *Fortune*, Mar. 20, 2000.

Serwer, Andy. "Travelers: Just Getting Started." *Fortune*, Oct. 27, 1997.

Sparks, Debra, and Grabarek, Brooke H. "1994 CEO of the Year Silver Award Winners." *Financial World*, Mar. 29, 1994.

# CHAPTER FOUR

# WILLIAM E. SIMON, JR.

## Manager, Private Equities Group

### WILLIAM E. SIMON & SONS

## A Prosecutor in the House

*One thing I learned [as a U.S. attorney] was to be thorough. The importance of asking a lot of questions. You can't ask too many questions, even if you annoy people. You do it in a nice way. You listen and you ask the next logical question. It's amazing how much you learn by just letting people talk. The other thing I learned was that people don't change much. Leopards don't change their spots....I wondered why that is. People get into habits. They get into certain ways of thinking, certain ways of behaving...so when we look at an investment opportunity, one of the most important things we try to assess is what kind of person are we dealing with.*

—WILLIAM E. SIMON, JR.

Say the words "merchant bankers," and one invariably conjures images of genteel elderly gentlemen sipping cognac from crystal glasses, smoking large cigars, and discussing matters of international trade. But William E. Simon & Sons is not your father's merchant bank—not entirely, that is. In fact, some of the principles that keep the company on track were learned in the process of prosecuting criminals with the U.S. attorney's office in New York City. But more on that later. First, let's look at some history:

The late William E. Simon, Sr., had a successful Wall Street career as a bond trader before joining the Nixon administration in 1973 as deputy secretary of the treasury. He was subsequently named director of the Federal Energy Office—the so-called energy czar—and served as secretary of the treasury in two administrations, under Presidents Nixon and Ford.

In the 1980s, he and partner Raymond G. Chambers (their company was Wesray) pioneered the concept of the leveraged buyout, purchasing more than 25 usually undervalued companies, generally with borrowed money, whipping them into shape and selling them at a profit. Among the companies they bought were such famous brands as Avis Rent-A-Car and Wilson Sporting Goods. Perhaps his most famous deal—and the one that started it all—was for Gibson Greeting Cards. Simon and Chambers bought the firm for $80.5 million in 1982 and took it public 14 months later, at a profit of $70 million to each of them.

Simon's partnership with Chambers ended in 1986, and two years later he founded William E. Simon & Sons, which currently has four major divisions:

- The Realty Group, which invests in real estate, both domestically and overseas—hotels, apartments, land development, and the like. Its present value is about $1.5 billion.

- The Capital Markets Group, which manages funds and investments. It also is a full-service municipal bond firm that underwrites markets and sells municipal bonds in primary and secondary markets.

- Special Situations Group, which manages the firm's fund for distressed debt—bank, private, and public—as well as leveraged equity investments.

- Private Equities Group, which, in many ways, is the most interesting of the four divisions. It's part venture capital fund, part miniconglomerate, acquiring companies in several core industries, such as moving, cabinetmaking, and metal products. Typically, Simon & Sons will buy one company in a core industry and then grow in some measure organically, but largely through acquisitions.

These companies are far more blue collar than gen-teel. Yet the strategy devised by the firm has built the Private Equities group to where it has a controlling interest or a significant investment in companies with an aggregate annual revenue of more than $2.2 billion.

The son of William E. Simon & Sons who manages the group is William, Jr., the former prosecutor, and between bites of breakfast at a genteel New York City hotel, the conversation centers on how that job helped make him a better M&A guy.

Simon had been a young attorney with a small litigation firm, hoping, as do all young lawyers, to get court time, but spending most of his hours doing the legal equivalent of grunt work. But he became involved in a high-profile case and was able to add that to his résumé, which impressed the people at the U.S. attorney's office for the southern district, which covers New York City.

Simon says, "That's a great job. To be an assistant U.S. attorney in New York City is a great job."

The link between fighting crime and acquiring businesses might seem tenuous at first to all but cynics, but the lessons Simon learned in the attorney's office have stood him in good stead building his company.

---

## LESSONS LEARNED AS A FEDERAL D.A.

"One thing I learned was to be thorough, the importance of asking a lot of questions, " Simon said. "You can't ask too many questions, even if you annoy people. If you do it in a nice way, [as] you [the author] are doing with me. You listen and ask the next logical question. It's amazing how much you learn by just letting people talk."

His experiences there also made him a little less trustful of people. "The other thing I learned was that people don't change much. Leopards don't change their spots—that type of analogy. The way I learned that was that you'd see people who'd lived a life of crime, and [after serving lengthy prison terms] they'd still always go back and do something else [illegal].

"You think if you commit a crime and go to jail, which is not a pleasant experience, clearly, and then get out of jail, you'd try to live an upstanding life. Well, most people don't. Why is that? I wonder why that is. It just became evident to me that people get into habits.

"They get into certain ways of thinking, certain ways of behaving. So when we look at investment opportunities, one of the most important things we assess is what kind of person we are dealing with—what kind of people are we looking at here?"

Despite the extensive and varied portfolio of companies he's built, most are small by conglomerate standards—in the $50 million to $500 million range in revenues. In many cases they are privately held, so judging the integrity of the owner or owners—getting a handle on how they conducted their business—is almost as important as studying the books.

"What I look for is honesty, candor, hard work, and some manner of intelligence," says Simon.

How does he determine what spots the leopard has on? "That's an area that's very difficult to make judgments about. Maybe some psychology courses teach it, but I'm not aware of any courses that talk about how to assess people....

"We'd have to meet a couple of times. Sure, there's a little bit of gut reaction involved. But I've been doing this for 12 years. And you get to a point where you get a sense once you spend some time with people. But, honestly, that sense can be dangerous. There are some people I know who say, 'I know inside of five minutes what a guy is like.' I'm not like that. And I'm also skeptical that you can know someone in five minutes.

"We're all very complicated people, and we're all the product of a lot of influences. So I'd have to get together with you on four or five or six occasions in different settings—something like this [a breakfast meeting] the first time. Then maybe we'd go to your place of work. I'd like to meet your family. I'd like to meet some of your friends. I'd like to spend time living with you, just you and I.

Beyond the normal due diligence a company conducts when it is planning a purchase, Simon tries to investigate the personalities of the people he's dealing with "almost every time. It depends on the investment. Sometimes we invest in publicly traded companies. We don't go to [that] extent [then]. But if it's a private investment, we spend a lot of time. Plus we do another thing I learned at the U.S. attorney's office, and that is the reference check.

"As much as you and I can spend four or five pleasant occasions together, there's no substitute for references. And that's not limited to the people you [list for] me. For example, you might say, 'I'll be happy to give you references. Here's [a list of] five people who know me.'

"I'll say, 'Great! But do you mind when I talk to those five people if I ask them for additional references? I'm not going to tell you who they are.'

"If you say, 'Check with me first. I don't want to bother these people,' I'll tell you, 'I understand your feelings, but I want to get some of these people cold.'"

Simon's skepticism has caused him to break off negotiations on more than one occasion. The most common red flag is "a lack of candor on the part of the executive.

"You're generally at some point going to find out a lot about the company. You're going to have your accountants [go in] and scrub it. You're going to meet the senior management. At some point, you're going to know a lot about the company, and if the information you have then is materially different from the information you were given [on] day one, that's a big red flag. Let's say—and this happened—that there's some kind of environmental problem that everybody in the company knows about, and they didn't bother to tell you about it for a month. You say, 'wait a minute.'

"Due diligence can cost anywhere from $10,000 to $300,000. At the company where we had environmental problems, at first the CEO said he didn't know about [them]. But the more we [spoke, we] realized he had to know and was lying about it, or he was incompetent. We were about $200,000 in, but that's cheap."

Simon's route to M&A started with his decision to become a lawyer, a choice he made in college. A history major and a regular reader of biographies, he read one about Clarence Darrow for a course and was mesmerized: "How he held audiences in sway and how he could speak in front of juries!"

---

# EARLY INFLUENCES

Until then, he'd been uncertain about his career path. Simon grew up in Summit, New Jersey, the oldest of seven children. Although his father became extremely wealthy on Wall Street, the family did not live an opulent lifestyle, and Simon worked growing up and while he was at Williams College. In fact, Simon claims the first time he had any idea exactly how rich his family was came when a college friend pointed out a story about his father's appointment to a government post in *The Wall Street Journal*. The story listed his father's earnings.

There is a commonly held belief that poor kids are scrappier than rich kids, who never had to fight for anything growing up. Simon believes that that is a myth. Though he never went hungry, "I've always been anxious to do well, to be successful. I've always had an ambition to do things properly, in a good way.... Sometimes I failed. I made mistakes. But by and large, I've tried to focus on things [at which] it seemed I had some ability."

Simon graduated from Williams College in 1973 and had visions of taking time off before law school to try the professional tennis tour. He'd played on the varsity team his four years in the school. However, his father convinced him to try a career in finance.

"Why don't you work in a bank," the senior Simon said. The two had been close, and Bill, Jr., said, "Why not. I'll give it a shot.

"I'd never given it much thought. I was a history major. But I said fine, and I went and interviewed at a bank in New York, and I ended up working there for six years."

It was the J. P. Morgan Bank, and the experience was in many ways as defining as the one he would have a few years later working for the Justice Department. "I went from being a history major in college to working in a great bank where you are exposed to lots and lots of influences and people. I went through the bank's training program with people who came from all over the country. Some people had been to business school. Lots of them had majored in economics. So for a while, I felt like I was [in] over my head."

The remedy became a characteristic of Simon's approach to business: "I just tried to work hard. It was kind of like the same as college. When I went there, there definitely were a lot of people smarter than I was. When I got to sports, one of the sports I played was squash. There were lots and lots of people who had played [before. I had just started playing it. So] I just had to work harder than them to get to the top of the ladder."

By his senior year, he made all-American in squash. He took the same approach in his new professional career.

"That's how I felt at Morgan. In order to hold my own—to be successful—because I didn't have the tools educationally or experientially, I had to work harder than anyone else."

He wound up in the foreign exchange department, which turned out to be an excellent training ground for his ultimate career in M&A. "In 1973 the foreign exchange area [of J. P. Morgan Bank] made $40 million, and the bank made $140 million. So basically we were responsible for a very significant percentage of the bank's earnings.

"We had 12 traders in our area, and I think 10 of them didn't go to college. So it was a wild and wooly area, and I enjoyed that. I was exposed to different countries, their economies, foreign exchange traders, and macroeconomic influences. I learned all about the major drivers of countries' economies, because they generally tend to vary with what the market thinks the country's currency is worth. Not to mention interest rates: I learned about what makes interest rates go up and what makes interest rates go down. It was a real course in economics—both from a macro sense and [from] a micro sense."

Periodically, he attempted to go back to law school, but every time he broached the subject to his bosses at J. P. Morgan, they threw a lot of money and/or additional responsibilities at him. He was clearly on a fast track for senior management, but after six years with the bank, he decided that it was now or never.

"I felt a little funny, to be honest. Morgan's a great bank, and [when I left] I felt a lot of people were thinking one of two things: Either he had to leave the bank—otherwise why would he be going back to school—[or] if he didn't have to leave the bank, he's even stupider than I thought." Simon laughs at his self-deprecating joke.

He went on to attend Boston College Law School and spent two years with the earlier mentioned New York City litigation firm and four as a prosecutor before joining his father and brother, J. Peter, in founding William E. Simon & Sons.

# THE REDCOATS ARE COMING! THE REDCOATS ARE COMING—WITH THEIR CHECKBOOKS!

Certainly, early on, the company was helped by Simon's father's reputation and connections. But the M&A division soon took on a life of its own. "At a certain point, you become known in the community and in the outside world as an entity that looks for companies. So you might get a cold call from someone. Other times you deal with investment bankers. We do business with business brokers."

Finding companies to purchase isn't difficult. "I liken it to the American Revolution. You know how we spotted the British because they were walking through the woods with red coats on and we were up in the trees? When we go looking for a company and we go walking through the woods with our checkbooks, we're like those redcoats."

Simon enters new industries in a variety of ways. Company executives may read something in a business journal about an industry that piques their interest. His M&A people spend a lot of time attending conferences and conventions in different industries. But very often, they learn about a business through that "redcoat visibility."

Once Simon finds an industry he believes to be viable, they do a standard investigation. "You study it, to make sure the drivers make good sense economically— supply, demand, all the traditional factors you look at in assessing whether an industry is attractive."

Perhaps the most important part of the process is to hire an expert in the field who can sift the wheat from the chaff among possible acquisitions. "They [acquisition candidates] all look good." Ideally, Simon finds someone who has extensive experience in an industry and has retired early or perhaps sold a company he or she owned and is now looking for fresh challenges and an equity interest in the company. They call it an executive-in-residence program.

"Take a person who has been with a cabinet company all his life. He's 45 years old. He was the CEO of a cabinet company. The company got sold. He wants to stay in the cabinet business, but he wants an ownership interest. So what he'll do is align himself with a firm like ours with just capital. It's great, because he knows the industry."

The executives in the executive-in-residence program come to Simon in a number of ways. In the late 1990s, Simon & Sons targeted B2B technology and searched for an executive to run that aspect of the business. When it couldn't find a qualified candidate on its own, it went with an executive search firm. "We were successful in finding someone, and he then went out and found an opportunity for us.

"What we don't try to do is invent it ourselves. We try to take advantage of other people's expertise. There are some people who say, if it's not invented here, I don't want to hear about it.' We're the reverse. We're totally open to letting other people come in the door [and] give us good ideas. [We] compensate them for it and try to build really good companies."

On the other hand, when Simon & Sons went into the metal-products area, it first found an executive—though quite by chance. "I got a call from Jack Kemp, who knew of a CEO in a metal-products company. The company had just been sold."

Kemp asked Simon to meet with him. Their meeting went well—better than well, in fact: "We had never looked at that industry before, and as a result of that phone call, we focused on the business."

One aspect of the firm's approach that is especially interesting is its flexibility. Often, companies involved in M&As have fixed rules about how they operate. With

Simon & Sons, it is less a matter of rules than generalizations to fit specific situations. Some companies will be absorbed; others will retain their identities.

For example, when the Bekins moving company became part of Simon & Son's GeoLogistics group (companies that, like Bekins, move people, but also freight forwarders that move packages around the world), Bekins had such good brand recognition, it would have been silly to tamper with it. "Do [people] wear Bekins shirts or GeoLogistics shirts? Well, they wear their Bekins T-shirts day in and day out. Customers know… Bekins."

---

# THE ACQUISITIVE CAT IN THE HAT

In some cases, Simon will buy an entire company. In other cases, he will take a majority interest. He will buy companies for the long term. He will buy for the short term. He will do it alone. He will do with partners. He will take companies public. He will keep companies private.

And if all this is starting to sound like a Dr. Seuss book, it's because, like Seuss books, the plot line is relatively simple: Do what fits the situation.

Certainly, there are guidelines. For one thing, the companies have to be profitable. The idea for Simon is not to turn around an unprofitable company, but to take a good company and make it better. "We've done both and based on our experience, it's better that a company be profitable."

For another, he also has to like the management. He doesn't have to love them, but he doesn't want an adversarial relationship. Simon & Sons deals primarily with midrange companies, up to $500 million. It's a size niche "we're comfortable with. There are a lot of big buyout firms out there that play in that top tier. We feel [that the midsize range] is a tier that is less competitive.

"In that size range, there's going to be a glitch of some kind. You're generally not going to have the greatest management [team]. Maybe you have a great CEO, but a mediocre CFO. Maybe you have a great CFO *and* a mediocre CEO. Maybe you have a need for MIS expertise. In some ways, we'll wind up strengthening management. We're in the business of trying to add value in addition to [using] our checkbook."

Simon & Sons also tries to stay away from unionized companies.

Simon & Sons allows the executives in residence to manage the companies independently. Because the firms often are in widely disparate industries, there aren't always clear-cut synergies, and even when there are synergistic possibilities, they are sometimes ignored.

"We own a company that consults in software design. So if [our] other companies needed software design, you would think...," and he lets his voice trail off into a soft chuckle. "But each of these companies [has its] own favorite software design companies. You can try. You can make the introduction."

But that's a minor irritant in what otherwise is a near-perfect way to make a living—at least as far as Simon is concerned. "This is a great business we're in. Maybe it's a unique point in history, but for a college graduate who majored in history and enjoys getting involved in different types of things—who likes to have variety, each day a little different, likes to have new challenges, learn new things—I really can't imagine any better activity to be involved in. You're always learning. It's full of surprises. It's just a terrific field to go into. I would encourage people to enter the buyout field."

## REFERENCES

Interview, William Simon, Jr., May 2000.

# CHAPTER FIVE

# HENRY R. KRAVIS
## Managing Partner

## KOHLBERG KRAVIS ROBERTS & CO.

## Making New Management Accountable—and Partners

*Management is an owner. Management has its own equity on the line. [Managers] have something at risk. I always like to refer to managers in corporate America as the renters of corporate assets, not the owners. Where have the Carnegies and the Mellons and the Rockefellers gone? A lot of them are gone. Our concept is bring back that ownership. If you have something at risk, you think differently....If you own the company, if you have your own money at risk, you start to say "Do we really need all those people? Do we need as many airplanes?"*

—HENRY R. KRAVIS

Henry Kravis and his leveraged-buyout firm, Kohlberg Kravis Roberts (KKR), exist as much because of the laws of physics as the laws of economics.

Nature abhors a vacuum, and that is where American business found itself in the early to mid-1970s. Somehow, someone or something had sucked the spirit from American enterprise. Gone was all semblance of leadership, of management skill, of vitality. In its place was a crumbling infrastructure, as unwieldy as it was old, bloated by unproductive workers left increasingly rudderless in a society that now looked to Asia for corporate innovation.

The combination of a global economy and deregulation created a newly competitive environment in which, sad as it may be, many American businesses were unequipped to participate. They were too slow footed, burdened by obsolescence, and too set in their ways.

It was in this atmosphere that KKR emerged to steer a movement that ultimately led to a rebirth of American business—and American business leadership. KKR took good companies and made them better, old firms and invigorated them, and turned around troubled companies.

KKR did this in part by requiring the management of the company it was acquiring to take an ownership stake (and outlook) in the business, paring down waste, investing in up-to-date technology, and freeing executives from worrying about the next quarter or even the next year. Suddenly, managers who had been prisoners of a Wall Street mentality were able to take long-range views.

Oh, and KKR made a bundle in the process.

KKR, of course, didn't change the American economy single-handedly. But it did show American businesspeople the possibilities—what could be done with the proper leadership and incentives. Just the *threat* of a takeover forced management to shake things up and reform.

## AT KKR, SUCCESS = LONG-RANGE THINKING

At its simplest, the KKR technique starts with finding an undervalued company. That doesn't merely mean that the firm's stock is low; in fact, early on, many of the companies KKR acquired were privately held. Instead, KKR was looking for companies that were underperforming—companies that could use a shot of adrenaline, a hit of modern management. The KKR methodology was as follows:

Typically, KKR purchased these companies using relatively little of its own resources. As much as 90 percent of the purchase price came in the form of "loans" (i.e., bonds, etc.). Instead of taking profits as dividends, KKR used the acquired company's cash flow to repay the debt, or it plowed the money back into the company. Profits—and they were substantial much more often than not—were taken two, three, or five years down the road, when the company was sold or taken public.

It is a process that has often been criticized. The leveraged-buyout (LBO) experts—and not just the KKR team—have been called robber barons, accused of being uncaring about the effect their deals had on working men and women. Certainly, there were times when an LBO was followed by layoffs and plant closings. But the LBO was not necessarily the *cause* of the layoffs. Slothful management *before* the LBO was frequently the problem; the layoffs were often the necessary cure. In fact, the KKR partners make the case that keeping people in inefficient or unproductive settings is not a virtue—that the layoffs and plant closings were the necessary cure. They argue, with considerable logic, that the long-term survival of a company ensures more, not fewer, jobs over that term.

But no matter which argument someone buys into, there's no denying that Kravis & Co. has changed the landscape of American business—for the better. It is now—to quote comedian Bill Murray in the film *Stripes*—a lean, mean fighting machine that is competitive the world over.

The man behind these changes grew up in Tulsa, Oklahoma, and might easily have gone into the petroleum business, like his father. That's certainly what his father, a well-known and well-respected engineer, wanted his son to do. "And I thought about it," Kravis told the Academy of Achievement shortly after he was inducted into its hall of fame.

"But I said, 'Look, as proud as I am of my father, I don't want to be known as Ray Kravis's son. I want to do something myself....' So I picked a field [in which] I had a little exposure—[in which] I thought I could have an enormous challenge and have a chance to really do some good, to be a pioneer in an area and not just be like everyone else."

After graduating boarding school on the east coast, Kravis attended Claremont McKenna College in California. But he spent summers back in New York working on Wall Street. "I started out as a runner, which was as a messenger," he said. "[In] my next [job,] I worked in the research department of Goldman Sachs, and my last summer I was in institutional and corporate sales."

He liked the idea of the financial potential—the big bucks—of corporate and institutional sales, but he didn't like the atmosphere. "I thought, 'when I am old (that meant 45 years of age), I want to have an office.' I didn't want to be at some desk, yelling and screaming[with] people hearing what I'm saying on the phone all the time."

From an atmospheric point of view, he was more attracted to the hallowed halls of corporate finance. Still, he was so intrigued by the idea of the "Big Deal," that he decided he wanted to find out how large institutions—the mutual funds that buy stocks and bonds—make their decisions.

"How did they make their decision to buy General Motors or IBM or whatever company it was," Kravis wondered. "I wanted to find out how the other side worked, because I didn't understand how one time an institutional salesman had a special on IBM and the next day he got a special on a block of stock on some other company—and another day another company."

# NOTHING BEATS ON-THE-JOB EXPERIENCE

So after graduation he went to work for Ed Merkle at the Madison Fund, a New York City–based, closed-end mutual fund. Merkle was a generous boss who threw Kravis into the fire just three weeks after he came on board. Merkle told him, "Kid, I want you to go call on a company called Tri-State Motor Transit in Joplin, Missouri."

When Kravis discovered he'd be on his own for the trip, he protested that it was too early in his career to be out in the field alone. Merkle disagreed, saying "There's no better way to learn than by trying."

This appealed to Kravis's nature. By his own admission, he was an average student who did well in courses he liked—political science, economics, finance—and not so well in those he didn't. "I was eager to learn everything I could. More important, I was eager to apply what I learned. That's why this job at the Madison Fund was so important to me. I look back at how much I really learned on the job. There is no substitute for on-the-job training."

The first thing Kravis learned was that you can't judge a book by its cover. He learned it when he landed at Joplin's airport and was greeted by a man in blue jeans who turned out to be the company's president. He was worth hundreds of millions of dollars, Kravis said, but he looked like the company driver.

After spending time with him, Kravis recommended buying Tri-State Motor Transit stock, which turned out to be a good decision. This was during the Vietnam War, and the company had a substantial number of contracts ferrying explosives. It's stock went up.

Another lesson Kravis learned was that preparation is everything. He was scheduled to meet with Roy Disney and was determined that his awe of the man not stand in the way. "That was a great experience for me, never having met anybody like that. I had read everything I could before I got there and had all my questions laid out. I had really thought through what I wanted to ask, and, as a result, it went well."

Things continued to go exceeding well for Kravis at the Madison Fund. Soon, he was not just recommending what stocks to buy—but what companies. Merkle told him, "Look, kid, you know how to pick stock. You buy a company the same way you buy stocks. If you don't like it, you just sell it. That's it."

Kravis continued at Madison while he worked on his MBA at Columbia University. But then he wound up at Bear Stearns, where his cousin, George Roberts, worked in the San Francisco office. There they perfected the techniques of what was then called a management buyout, but has since become known as the LBO.

"We probably bought seven or eight or nine different companies in the early seventies, culminating in the largest acquisition Bear Stearns did, which was in 1975," Kravis recalled. The company was called Incom International and was the industrial component group of Rockwell International. The cost was $92 million. "And Bear Stearns, I remember, got the biggest fee they'd ever gotten, which was $950,000."

When Kohlberg announced that he was leaving the company and offered to take the two cousins with him as junior partners, it was no surprise that Kravis jumped at the opportunity. For one thing, he had always been competitive. In fact, at boarding school, he ran track and was on the wrestling team because that meant "I didn't have to rely on anybody else. Nobody else [could] let me down. [I ran] as fast as I was going to be...and I wrestled as well as I could wrestle. If I lost, that was my own fault. I had nobody to blame but myself. That was something I learned in school. Don't look for excuses."

KKR opened shop May 1, 1976, and early on developed a set of fundamental rules that would become characteristic of its early acquisitions:

- The company had to have a good, predictable cash flow that would be sufficient to repay the new debt in a time frame that ranged from three to five years.

- In the beginning—this would change later on—there had to be good management in place. Very often, early on, the companies were family owned, with the owner facing estate problems. The family was generally kept on.

- And, though this would change later on, too, the deal had to be acceptable to the target companies' boards. Unfriendly takeovers didn't happen until much later.

- Finally, managers had to participate. They had to put up their own money. In fact, they were expected to invest a sizable portion of their personal wealth in the company, on the theory that owners are more alert to opportunities and less willing to spend money frivolously than managers who don't have an ownership position.

Kravis told the Academy of Achievement, "I think that's the reason we've been successful. It's not just buying the company. Sure, we pick the right companies, and we picked the right management, and, most importantly, we've given [managers] the right incentives to perform.

"Management is an owner. Management has its own equity on the line. [Managers have] something at risk. I always like to refer to managers in corporate America as the renters of corporate assets, not the owners. Where have the Carnegies and the Mellons and the Rockefellers gone? A lot of them are gone. Our concept is to bring back that ownership. If you have something at risk, you think differently....If you own the company, if you have your own money at risk, you start to say, 'Do we really need all those people? Do we need as many airplanes?'"

# BUYING A COMPANY AT THE RIGHT PRICE

Typically, incentives are tied both to a company's annual performance and to a three- to five-year bonus plan. Executives can double their salaries by meeting an array of goals set at the beginning of each year.

But even the world's best management can't make a deal work if it is priced wrong from the start. The hardest part of any deal was figuring out what to pay for a company. As George P. Baker and George David Smith point out in *The New Financial Capitalists*, their sympathetic examination of the KKR empire:

"Calibrating the price for a prospective buyout was a delicate matter. In order to convince the prospective (and often reluctant) sellers, premiums had to be paid over the current share prices; but the success of any buyout required that buyers not overpay. Balancing these conflicting pressures required enough discipline to walk away from very tempting prospects that were even slightly overpriced based on conservative forecasts of what the projected debt service would require."

Kravis agrees:

"It's one of the most important things at the end of the day, being able to say 'no' to an investment— even if you've done a lot of work. Work will never hurt you. But once you buy a company, you are married. It's not like Ed Merkle said, 'If you don't like it, just sell it.' It's a lot harder to sell a company than it is to buy it....

"People always call and congratulate us when we buy a company. I say, 'Look, don't congratulate us when we buy a company. Congratulate us when we sell it.' Because any fool can overpay and buy a company, as long as the money will last to buy it. Our job really *begins* the day we buy the company and start working with management. We start working with where this company is headed."

---

# A TYPICAL DEAL

How does the usual deal work? Although it very likely was different each time, Baker and Smith came up with a good rule-of-thumb kind of example. Consider a company purchased for $100 million—$10 million cash and the rest in debt. The company had been generating a cash flow of $10 million, or the equivalent of a 10-percent return. But, through improvements in its operations, better management of assets, or a host of upgrades KKR typically introduces, cash flow doubles to $20 million a year. KKR doesn't take dividends, and the entire $20 million is used for debt service.

This company can repay the entire $90 million (assuming a 10 percent interest rate) in about six years. At that time, even if the company is still worth only $100 million, KKR's initial $10 million investment is now worth $100 million—or a *compounded annual rate of return of about 47 percent*.

Of course, not every deal works out so smoothly. The unexpected, however, is exactly what appeals to Kravis. "I love the creativity. I love the ability to create a capital structure that is appropriate for a company, no matter what field it happens to be in."

Consider the creativity that was applied when KKR purchased Fred Meyer, Inc., a chain of 65 retail stores (general merchandise and food items) that also owned a dairy, a bakery, a photofinishing plant, and a pharmaceutical plant. To work the financing out, Fred Meyer was split into two separate entities: the Real Estate Group and the Acquisitions Corporation.

The real estate—primarily the land under the stores—had been leased under terms below current market value, in effect serving as a considerable subsidy. The leases were renegotiated to reflect the day's values more accurately, which resulted in several immediate benefits.

First, with the real estate's value and leases revalued upwards, the real-estate company could shoulder a larger portion of the debt, making it easier to arrange financing. The real-estate end of the business was pur-

chased for $304 million, compared to the $229 million
spent for the stores themselves.

Second, with the real estate now valued to reflect
true market rates and with leases generating market-
level income, the possibility was opened that some or all
of the real estate could be sold to raise cash.

Finally, without a real-estate subsidy to artificially
raise their profits, store managers had to rethink their
priorities. Stores that were marginal with the subsidy
were now closed, and managers could spend time and
effort concentrating on improving operations and profits in the remaining stores.

It was, Baker and Smith point out, "never enough to
ascertain that a company's stock was undervalued. It was
important to form a clear picture of where and how
value could be unlocked."

In a similarly creative vein, KKR partnered with
Allied Signal (KKR's first joint venture) when it purchased an Allied Signal subsidiary, Union Texas Petroleum (UTP). The deal was structured in such a way as to
protect KKR from the vagaries of the oil market. Oil was
selling for $35 a barrel at the time (1984), but, less than
a year later, was down to just $10 a barrel. Thanks to the
way the deal was done (in a manner best understood by
accountants), not only was KKR's investment protected,
but UTP still had access to funds to pay off the debt,
despite the price volatility of oil.

Again, according to Baker and Smith, "They crafted
financial structures based on cautious projections of
cash flows and made those structures as flexible as possible. They looked for margins of safety in every investment and anticipated alternative plans for generating
cash should that be necessary."

If there is no common pattern to the way KKR arranges its financing, there certainly is in the attitude KKR brings to its new partner. Talk about the vagaries of the oil market, consider the vagaries of the stock market and the pressures it applies for quarter after quarter of gains. Inevitably, Wall Street forces managers to think for the short term rather than for the greater corporate good. KKR's counsel is "We want to build value over time. We're in this for the long haul, and that requires patience.

"The trouble with America today is that everything is thought of in [fiscal] quarters. [On the other hand], we say to the management of companies, you are here today. Where do you want to be five years from now, and how are you going to get there? It may very well mean taking a step backwards, but believe me, in five years we are going to have a company that is much more productive, efficient, and competitive."

Consider Robert Kidder, who was the head of Duracell when KKR purchased it from Kraft. He had some reservations after the acquisition: He and fellow managers were afraid that the new owners would cut capital investments as a way to help pay off the debt. Their fears proved groundless.

In fact, under KKR, Duracell could move faster. "My capital authority during the Kraft era—and keep in mind that this is a $1.1 billion company and I was being paid a lot of money to run the business," Kidder said, "was $250,000, ridiculouly low. The day after the LBO became official, my authority became everything up to $5 million before it goes to the board—and this in a time of those tightly controlled LBOs. Suddenly we became liberated."

# MANAGERS ARE GIVEN RESPONSI-BILITY—AND THE AUTHORITY AND FREEDOM TO DO THE JOB

Interestingly, Kravis applies this same thinking to KKR. Employees are allowed—and indeed encouraged—to buy into any deal the company closes. The amount they are permitted to invest depends upon their seniority. In addition, all senior partners share in the bonus pool, regardless of whether they've initiated or closed any deals in the year. As with the employees of the companies KKR owns, it wants its own people to think long term.

KKR also practices what it preaches in terms of getting (or, for that matter, keeping) good managers in place at companies it acquires and then letting them manage. Having turned managers from custodians of corporate resources to owners, KKR leaves operational decisions to them and focuses on monitoring the firm's financial performance and long-term strategies. According to Baker and Smith, "KKR's prime responsibilities were to watch over its companies on a close and continuous basis, to help structure executive compensation, to intervene in [a] timely fashion when management ran into serious problems, and to engineer corporate refinancings, acquisitions, and divestitures....The firm's standing in the capital markets helped to lower the cost of capital to its constituent companies, and its intimate knowledge of their ongoing financial needs enabled it to restructure debt, issue capital stock, and otherwise make timely and efficient changes in capital structure."

A related point is that Kravis believed in doing business honorably. KKR partners knew there were no shenanigans. As James B. Stewart pointed out in *Barbarians at the Gate*, his account of the behind-the-scenes maneuvers in the battle for RJR Nabisco, one of the book's principals, Martin Siegel of Drexel Burnham, faced prison time for enriching himself and several friends while serving as an outside adviser to KKR. Although he readily gave the law the names of coconspirators to avoid prison, he couldn't give the prosecutors what they wanted, namely, Henry Kravis's head on a platter, because Kravis had done nothing illegal.

Consider how KKR reacted when it ran into difficulties with a company called EFB trucking. The firm was created by a merger of FB Trucking, a Utah-based carrier, and Eagle Trucking, which the KKR partners had owned since their days at Bear Stearns. A combination of factors including deregulation and higher fuel prices, created a negative cash flow for EFB.

The expedient way to handle the problem was to declare bankruptcy and let a federal judge deal with the details. Instead the company assigned a partner full time to liquidate the trucking company, sell its assets, and adjudicate its liabilities, at a considerable cost in time and energy. As Baker and Smith note, "Bankruptcy was sometimes useful, but only after other alternatives were exhausted. It was in KKR's interest to try everything feasible to make its lenders whole short of bankruptcy." The partner's efforts resulted in higher returns for creditors than bankruptcy would have—and bred trust in potential future partners.

In the early years, KKR had the LBO field pretty much to itself. But inevitably, success brought competition, which forced the prices KKR had to pay for companies higher and higher and increased competition for financing as well. However, because of KKR's reputation—for making money and for integrity—getting funds was usually not a problem.

Kravis expects those same high standards in his employees. "I'm looking for people who are bright and who have the highest ethical standards. I will not compromise one iota on that. I want people who will stand up to me, even though what they're saying is probably not what I want to hear."

To make sure that his people don't just say what they think he wants to hear, Kravis starts meetings by getting the opinions of junior members of the staff first. "Everything comes from the bottom up. I have a very good interchange. We'd always be the last, George [Roberts] and I, to say what we thought. So it's not a directive saying 'We will buy this company. Run the numbers and prove that we are doing the right thing.' It's 'Should we buy it? What do you think?'"

What keeps Kravis motivated after all these years? Fear? Yes, fear: "We have fear all the time. But that's what keeps us going. That's what keeps us focused. People who say 'I have no fear. I'm not afraid of failing' are kidding themselves. Sometimes it's the fear of failure, not wanting to fail, that makes a lot of people as great as they are. I know that's what pushes me a lot."

# REFERENCES

Anders, George. "KKR's Leverage—Merchants of Debt." *Economist*, June 13, 1992.

Baker, George P., and Smith, George David. *The New Financial Cap-

*italists: Kohlberg Kravis Roberts and the Creation of Corporate Value*. New York: Cambridge University Press, 1998.

Castro, Janis. "Big-Time Buyouts Duel of the Takeover Titans." *Time*, Nov. 7, 1988.

Donohue, Christine. "At RJR Nabisco, New Owner KKR Is Already Wielding the Knife." *Marketing Week*, Aug. 21, 1989.

Girard, Keith F. "Profiles in Power." *Business Month*, May 1989.

Hylton, Richard T. "How KKR Got Beaten at Its Own Game." *Fortune*, May 2, 1995.

Interview of Henry R. Kravis with Academy of Achievement, Feb. 1991.

Loomis, Carol J. "Buyout Kings." *Fortune*, July 4, 1988.

Moore, Thomas. "KKR Is Rolling with the Punches." *U.S. News & World Report*, May 7, 1990.

Mulligan, John W. "KKR, Member FDIC." *Institutional Investor*, June 1991.

Newcomb, Peter, and Lataniotis, Delores. "Kravis/Roberts." *Forbes*, Oct. 13, 1997.

Sellers, Patricia. "The New Siege at RJR Nabisco." *Time*, Feb. 8, 1993.

# CHAPTER SIX

# CHARLES WANG
## Chairman
### COMPUTER ASSOCIATES

# My Way or the Highway

*We try to place as many people as we can. We interview all of the [employees of the firms we acquire]. We rank them by the ones we think are the best. We try to judge their character. Don't forget, during that interview, that person is going to be the best he can be. If he has a chip on his shoulder—if he has an attitude—we've got a problem with this guy. And we've had people who were just obnoxious. Okay, fine. Then go do something else with your career. Computer Associates is nothing but a train of opportunities. You get on or you don't get on. The train is leaving the station. We're gonna go on. Nobody should believe that they're the most crucial thing. Not me. Not anybody. It's got a life of its own. The train's pulling out. Jump on board, have some fun, make a lot of money. Or stay off it and get out of the way.*

—CHARLES WANG

Charles Wang doesn't look nearly as fierce as his reputation.

Wang (pronounced Wong) strides purposely into a conference room at Computer Associates (CA) International's dazzling headquarters building in the New York City suburb of Islandia. The megawatt smile on his face is big enough to power a mainframe. And his company, though far less well known than giants such as Microsoft, is big enough to provide the software that helps 95 percent of the Fortune 500 run their computers.

Wang started CA in 1976. Early on, the company was financed by the well-known venture capital firm of Visa & Master Card. Now it is a $6 billion megalith. Wang grew CA with a single-minded, almost ferocious dedication and loyalty to his company—he's been called ruthless— and a shrewd combination of internal growth and acquisitions. Today it is a far cry from its humble beginnings.

"When we first opened, we had one goal, and that was to survive to the next week," Wang recalls about CA's early days. He and cofounder Russell Artzt, a college buddy, spent almost as much time scouring for new credit cards to help them pay their bills as selling and developing products.

"If we got to the next week, we were so happy. We thought we were brilliant people: We bought ourselves one more week. At the end of the year, we start[ed] to think [in bigger terms], 'Well, we bought ourselves a month.'"

It's clear as he says this that he relishes the memories, almost as much as he enjoys thinking about how far he's come. "Now," he adds, "we know that this company has a life of its own. With or without me, it will go on. It's a big company. It's a good company, and the foundation is right."

Wang built the foundation by concentrating on the basics—on serving one market, the business market, and serving it well. Computer Associates makes and services the platform software that works behind the scenes in business computers—to schedule work, to provide security, and for storage. "We're the plumbing, not the fixtures," he says repeatedly in describing his products. "We're the ones that give you the platform that allows you to be up and running, and so that it's secure, so that you can manage it, so that you can build the application."

Once the foundation was established, Wang achieved his crowning glory: relatively seamlessly integrating various companies—including over 200 acquisitions—under the CA banner. More important, he has been able to bring in their different product lines and create a whole greater than the sum of its parts.

In one sense, Wang's achievements are a validation of the American dream, a kind of Horatio Alger story. He was born in Shanghai in 1944 into a prosperous family. His father was a judge, and the family had spacious quarters in the wealthy French quarter of the city, both of which immediately made the family suspect following the Communist takeover in 1949. The signs of impending trouble were all around.

"You know you have to leave when all your friends are going to jail for different things," Wang says, speaking in a voice that still carries faint traces of a Chinese accent. "You know it's not cool to stay here anymore."

Wang's father escaped first, climbing through barbed wire into Hong Kong. Wang's mother, he, and his two brothers followed in almost comical fashion. "My mother basically said to the state authorities, 'There's no way I can support myself and the boys. I want to go get that husband who left me. How dare he go.'"

Either the bureaucrats fell for her line, were glad to get rid of the family, or were otherwise preoccupied, because they told her to go, and let her take the children with her. The Wangs stayed with family in Hong Kong for about six months, during which time the senior Wang found a job in the United States, teaching international law at St. John's University in Queens, New York. So the family set off again, first by boat to Hawaii. While Charles's father flew the rest of the way to make preparations, Charles, his mother, and his two brothers took the boat to San Francisco and then a train to New York. "We couldn't afford to fly," Wang says with a grin. "It wasn't like we had Advantage Miles. There was no such thing."

# DIFFICULTY ADJUSTING—AT FIRST

It was 1952, Charles was just eight years old, and, as it turned out, he needed to adjust to his new home. For one thing, the family's economic circumstances were sharply diminished. When Charles first saw the apartment building in which his family would live, he was disappointed to discover that the entire building wasn't theirs—just a small section of it.

He was also placed back a year at school at first, from third to second grade. "I didn't understand what was going on. They didn't think I was very bright. So they moved me back. That's pretty humiliating, for a kid all of a sudden to go back with smaller kids."

Finally, unlike China, the United States is far from a homogeneous country. Young Wang suddenly had to deal with being different and the prejudice that seems to come with that. The Wangs were the only Asian family in the area, and Charles was the subject of hurtful taunts from other children—"you know how kids grab their eyes"—and out-and-out prejudice from adults. When the Wangs tried to buy their first house, a neighborhood family circulated a petition urging the owners not to sell to them.

Pop psychologists might suggest that it was a combination of these factors that spurred Wang on to maximum achievement. But he attributes his success to something far more prosaic: "I think the most important factor was being the second born, the middle sibling. You learn to compromise, to protect your younger brother from your older brother. Also, in a Chinese family, the sun rises and sets on the firstborn son. He's going to carry on the family name, blah, blah, blah. The younger one is the baby. So as a middle sibling, you think you're getting the short end of the stick.

"But the second son is a little more free. So it builds a different kind of character than if you're the oldest or the youngest. For me, family position is very important—even though I think my mother loved me more than the others."

Wang lets out a guffaw and adds, "Yes, that's on the record. And I love her more than any other mother."

Wang denies published reports that he was a mediocre student at Queens College. "I wouldn't say mediocre," he claims. "I would say poor. Mediocre is very complimentary."

He majored in math and decided not to pursue an advanced degree after graduating in 1966. "I didn't think I could do it." Also, he had no idea what he wanted to do—although he had no doubt that whatever it was, he'd be successful.

"I always used to tell my brothers, 'You guys are much smarter than I am. Your SAT scores are better. Your IQs are higher. But I can outwork both you guys. If I have to, I'll work all day, all night. I won't sleep. I'll do whatever it takes' I can outwork [anyone,] and that, my friend, is basically the business."

---

# HE FOUND A CAREER IN
## *The New York Times*

Where to begin? Wang checked the help-wanted ads and saw pages upon pages of advertisements for computer programmers. For Wang, that represented a kind of security. So he thought he'd give it a try. He applied for, and got, a programmer trainee position at Columbia University. "When I wrote my first program, I said, 'This is it. I know what I want to do.'"

He followed four years at Columbia with a succession of software sales jobs. In 1974 a small Swiss software company, Computer Associates, signed him up as U.S. distributor of a program that sorted and merged data on mainframes.

Artzt has said that his partner-to-be had a simple sales technique: "He'd pick 20 pages out of the Yellow Pages, drink three cups of coffee, and not go to the bathroom until he'd cold-called every potential customer."

Understandably, given that level of dedication, the U.S. operation was so successful that it soon became the tail wagging the dog. In 1976, Wang and Artzt bought the company. Despite Wang's determination, early on, CA's future was touch and go. The computer business— at least as we know it today—was still in its infancy. A sizable number of information technology executives preferred to write programs themselves. Purchasing off-the-shelf software was not only not de rigueur; it wasn't even cool.

Equally problematic was that a good percentage of the software written at that time was more clever than functional. Wang imagines a common conversation between programmers and company executives that might have taken place then:

*Programmer:* Look at this program. Isn't it neat?

*Executive:* What would we use it for?

*Programmer:* I don't know, but, boy, isn't it neat?

Finally, even the most savvy CEOs at the time tended to see computers as tools for taking over repetitive manual processes—billing and mailings, for example— rather than tools for eliminating problems in scheduling and inventory and the dozens of other tasks computers routinely handle today.

The turning point for Wang came when he recognized that if CA was to grow, it couldn't sell software—or at least it couldn't sell software alone. It had to sell the *benefits* of the software. He was prescient in understanding that, ultimately, businesspeople need solutions rather than clever computer code. Although that sounds obvious now, it wasn't so apparent at the time. The urge to be clever wasn't limited to corporate IT programmers. The high-tech world is littered with the remnants of companies that became enamored with the technology, to the detriment of the business.

"Suppose you and I want to go to the airport," Wang explains. "If we ask a technical person how to get there, he'll tell you how to build a car. And that's still the fundamental problem in our industry. The industry is still so young that it's being driven by technical people who want to build cars. But my problem as a business[person] is a transportation problem. I need to get from here to there. It's not a manufacturing problem. I don't want to build cars. I want to just get in and drive to my destination."

# ONLY THREE REASONS TO ACQUIRE ANOTHER COMPANY

In the same way that CA's initial growth came by concentrating on creating practical software solutions to real-world business problems, the firm continued to grow through Wang's insistence on staying practical. He eschewed acquisitions that might enhance the bottom line, but not the product line. He resisted the temptation to acquire companies that served Wall Street expectations for immediately higher earnings, but did not necessarily serve the needs of his customers.

Almost all CA acquisitions share a bond: a Thomas Paine–like commonsense approach to expansion. There are, claims Wang, only three reasons to buy another company: to acquire technology, to get key people, and to add a new client base—or, very often, a combination of the three. These simple, clear-cut standards eliminate many companies as acquisition candidates. As a result, CA is spared the difficult task of integrating two companies that don't fit—the equivalent of putting together a single picture puzzle of different scenes. While integrating two companies is never simple, it's certainly a lot easier when you know that all the pieces are supposed to fit.

In many ways, the decision whether to buy a company in order to get hold of its technology is the easiest, Wang claims. The top CA executives—Wang himself, CA President and CEO Sanjay Kumar, and research director Artzt—all have technical backgrounds. "We know what it takes to write something," Wang maintains, referring, of course, to writing a computer program. "If need be, we'll sit down and write it ourselves. We know how many iterations you go through before it becomes a real product, not just a prototype.

"So if we're interested in a program that another company developed, when we talk to that company, we know what's real and what's not. We also know what it would take for us to develop it if we did it ourselves. This way, we can weigh several factors: How fast do we want to get to the marketplace with it? What will it take for me to do it myself? [and does the other company] bring a new client base to the mix? Then we evaluate what the value of the company is to us. But we can do that only if we understand what it is to write code."

For example, in 1995 Wang spent $2.8 million to purchase Legent, a Herndron, Virginia-based computer company that created several systems management tools. "Everybody thought it was all because of this mainframe stuff [the software programs Endeavor and Paradigm]. But all we were really interested in was Agent Works, [which had] one piece of code I wanted for Unicenter."

Agent technology involves small components that sit in a machine and perform various tasks on the user's behalf. For example, the software will remember what a user is looking for and let him or her know when it finds it. Agent was incorporated into CA's Unicenter TNG program, which monitors and manages the health of corporate computer systems, and enabled Wang to bring this innovative product to market much earlier.

"It would have taken us a year or two years to develop it, and we knew we needed it right away. But they had no idea of the value of what they had, because they never wrote code."

Beyond technology, as noted, Wang is also attracted to companies by their customer base. Because of the wide range of products it offers, Wang is convinced that CA can sell up the acquired company's clients—that is, it can improve and modernize their existing software, sell new products, and, of course, add lucrative service contracts. CA's acquisitions can be, in effect, as *Business Week* put it, "a launch pad into new markets."

Wang also is attracted by a first-rate team of programmers: "A company could have a good technology team that wasn't properly focused by management on what to develop."

The process of acquiring other companies has become easier now, in part because practice makes perfect and in part because the system seems to work. "When you do an acquisition the first time, and you say here's what we're going to do, the people [i.e., CA employees] all fight it. They say, 'We're not sure.' The second acquisition comes and the people still aren't sure. But come the tenth, those people who were there for the first and the second or third—they know it works."

CA's rapid growth has not come without controversy. A 1997 *Fortune* magazine article entitled "Tough Guys Finish First"suggested that "Wang has built his empire aided by a ruthless formula: He buys flagging software rivals...immediately fires people, and then cuts costs until profits pile up." Since CA was boasting over 50-percent annual shareholder returns at the time, the presumption is that *Fortune* meant *ruthless* in the nicest way.

Certainly, there is some truth to the magazine's description of Wang's M.O. What's lacking is depth. In many cases, some of the companies, such as Applied Data Corporation and Ask Group, were flagging. So? If Wang hadn't bought them, who knows what future—if any—these companies might have had.

---

## NOW DEALS—AND DEAL MAKERS— COME TO COMPUTER ASSOCIATES

There are more examples for skeptics: At Cullinet, a company in the red when CA acquired it in 1989, four

executives had bought themselves corporate Range
Rovers. Legent had three separate headquarters. Wang
told *Fortune* magazine: "We could have fit 10 people in
the CEO's office."

As Wang's reputation as an acquisitionist grew,
he became a magnet for deals and deal makers, particularly people hawking companies that were, well,
troubled.

"They become available," he notes. "You don't have to
look for them. They come to you. A large percentage of
them. We know the competition. We know the marketplace. We know who has what. We know this will fit. This
won't fit. And if the opportunity is right, why not take
advantage of it?"

By "opportunity," Wang means that the acquired
company brings something to the table that ultimately
will help CA or its customers.

In most cases, acquired management favors the
deal. With typical candor, Wang explains why: "They've
already worked out with their boards all the wonderful
benefits. They'll have their severance packages. They
take good care of themselves. You never have to cry
for those managers. They do very well for themselves."
But even executives initially opposed to merging often
see the golden parachute at the end of the rainbow.
Top executives from acquired companies rarely make
the transition to CA. "This dragon has only one head,"
is the way Wang frequently explained his policy.

Working things out below the top-management level,
though, becomes a little trickier. One of Wang's first purchases, in 1989, was a company called Capex. He wanted
to adopt the Capex bookkeeping system at CA, but was
told it would take nine programmers half a year to do it.

Wang tackled the job on a red-eye and came up with a rough, but working, program literally overnight. That set the tone at Capex. Wang told *Business Week* that he didn't fire anyone because of the incident—but he didn't have to: "People started quitting. The Capex people were very different from us culturally." Today, Wang refuses to allow a foreign nine-programmers, six-months type of culture to invade CA.

"We do what is necessary to be sure the business goes on," Wang explains. "We never had a reduction in force—a layoff—[at CA] since I started the company. My loyalty is to my people. When I acquire a company, I tell everybody in that company what [their] future is [with CA]. If I don't see a future for you, I'm going to tell you, because I owe it to you. I can't have you make an investment in a career here if I know I'm going to close your department or do something else [that will affect you adversely].

"At the same time, I don't think it's right for CA to invest in you when we know it's a dead end. I don't need two legal departments, so I'm going to tell the lawyers that we acquired, 'Listen, guys, you have no future. We've worked out a severance package for you, so let's go. Okay? We'll work with you to be sure you have placement, and so on.' And I tell every one [at] the same time. This way there are no lingering doubts, no waiting for the second and third shoe to drop. For the people who are left, we assimilate them right away. They become part of Computer Associates.

"Obviously, for some reason, people go ahead and say this is so brutal. But every CEO we speak to always says, 'Charles, that's the way to do it. It's the right way to do it. I just can't do it myself.'"

# ALL ABOARD FOR THE RIDE OF A BUSINESS LIFETIME

Because it has engendered a modicum of controversy, the subject of employee retention comes up several times during a conversation. Later, Wang says:

"We may not need the finance department, but we may still want the people there. We try to place as many people as we can. We interview all of the [employees from the acquired company]. We rank them by the ones we think are the best. We try to judge their character. Don't forget, during that interview, that person is going to be the best he can be. If he has a chip on his shoulder—if he has an attitude—we've got a problem with this guy. And we've had people who were just obnoxious. Okay, fine. Then go do something else with your career. Computer Associates is nothing but a train of opportunities. You get on or you don't get on. The train is leaving the station. We're gonna go on. Nobody should believe that they're the most crucial thing. Not me, not anybody. It's got a life of its own. The train's pulling out. Jump on board, have some fun, [and] make a lot of money. Or stay off it and get out of the way."

People who do get on the train are frequently in for the rides of their lives. Wang is a benevolent boss. He offered CA employees gyms and day care centers long before such benefits were de rigueur in the computer industry. "Our jobs as executives and [managers] is to provide an environment so that the company can grow. We do everything we can to create that environment."

On the surface, that sounds like public relations puff, but the proof of Wang's pudding is in CA's executive roster: Sanjay Ragi, the company's president and new CEO, was with Ucell. Doug Robinson, chief financial officer of a recent CA spinoff, was with Cullinet, a 1989 merger partner. Even Bob Gordon, who heads public relations and set up my interview with Wang, came with the acquisition of Applied Data Research in 1988.

There are, Wang says, three steps in creating the kind of employee environment he promotes:

"You [the employees] have got to feel that what you contribute to your group is important in some way. You could be a secretary or you could be a programmer, but you've got to feel that what you're doing will have an effect on the company.

"Second, you're gonna be paid very well. My people are all overpaid. I pay them very well. I do. For example, our options go to 60 percent of the people at Computer Associates. Sixty percent of the people have options. So they're riding with it. They're building something.

"The third thing that companies seem to forget is that you've got to have fun doing this. You've got to create the atmosphere where people can fail. If you fail, learn from it and go on. Don't spend all your time spinning about who did what. Just say, 'I screwed up. What did I learn from this? How do I avoid that in the future?'"

Wang believes that new employees pick up on the it's-okay-to-take-a-risk culture from the ambience of Islandia. "You gotta have an atmosphere that says if you screw up it's okay. But don't screw up on the same thing [again]. That's stupid. You screwed up. What did you learn from it?"

He adds that employees know when they fail. "I tell them. And then I say, 'Let's not spend time spinning about it, because as soon as you start spinning, you've got a problem with me.'"

He encourages his people to think outside the box, telling them to stand on their heads when they look at a problem

Gradually, new people acquire the CA way. "They see the people around them who have come here through acquisitions—they see the opportunity. And they become part of CA."

If CA generally and Wang in particular are so benevolent, why do people say nasty things about them? Wang maintains that part of the negative rhetoric comes from employees of acquired companies who didn't make the cut at CA. "When we acquire a company and, let's say, there are 20 people we don't need, they go to a competitor. They'll never say 'I'm just not good enough [to be hired by CA]. So CA becomes all the bad things—whatever they want to say."

There's no question that Wang is a hard-nosed competitor, and that has engendered some ill will. Wang even sues his clients. One of his customers, Newport News Shipbuilding, claims that CA threatened to shut down Newport's computers. Wang sued EDS, CA's largest customer, charging that it violated its licensing agreement.

Wang makes no apologies: "These companies with big purchasing departments don't get it. You don't *buy* the software; you license it to use under certain circumstances. It's almost like when you go to Blockbuster to rent a videotape. If you take that video and charge admission to see it in Madison Square Garden, you've got problems. Right? You didn't buy [the tape]. You licensed...it [to be used] only under certain circumstances: only for your home use, not for profit.

"Purchasing departments don't think that way. Big companies think they purchased the software. They don't get it. So we end up in big fights with them, because the only thing we have is this intellectual property called software. We're not an IBM, which can say, 'Okay. We won't charge you for it. We'll just put the cost into the hardware.' We can't do that. We're not Microsoft, which has a monopoly (which the government has shown)."

---

# SUCCESS CHANGES PEOPLE'S OPINIONS

Whether it's because of his longevity or his success, some harsh opinions of Wang have turned to grudging respect and admiration. Larry Ellison, the chief executive officer at Oracle Corporation called Wang "the scavenger" of the software ecosystem in 1996. Today he tells *Business Week* that Wang "has done a great job in operations—a spectacular job. We could learn from that."

Similarly, at one time Andrew Filipowski, CEO of Platinum Technologies International, Inc., said he'd rather close his company than sell to Wang. Today Platinum is part of CA, and Filipowski says he didn't really mean it. "It's the same as Sun and Microsoft and Coke and Pepsi. You've got to present an arch rivalry to the investment community."

Wang, too, has mellowed. He's called the EDS suit "stupid." He told *Communications Week*, "There are things we could have done probably a little smoother.

The way we worked with customers was misunderstood. We felt very strongly about the sanctity of contacts, and sometimes, to prove this point, we became dead right....I think that cost us."

Overall though, Wang is the Frank Sinatra of CEOs: "I don't look back and say I wish I'd done something this way or that. I don't live my life that way. I play as hard as I can. I have great fun and always look forward. If you look backwards at the could haves and should haves and would haves, you'll have a miserable life. There's always something you could have done better, something you could have done differently. You can't undo it."

# REFERENCES

Bianco, Anthony. "Software's Tough Guy." *Business Week*, Mar. 6, 2000.

Bull, Katherine, and Fitzloff, Emily. "Computer Associates' Charles Wang Sheds Light on Product Strategy." *InfoWorld*, May 18, 1998.

Cortese, Amy. "Sexy? No. Profitable, You Bet." *Business Week*, Nov. 11, 1996.

Dalton, Richard J. Computer Associates in $3.5 Billion Deal." *Newsday*, Mar. 30, 1999.

Gillooly, Varyn, and Foley, John. "Chaos Theory—Computer Associates Is Shifting Its Product Line to Help Sort Out Customers Mixed IT Environments." *Information Week*, Apr. 27, 1998.

Girishankar, Saroja. "CA: Putting All the Pieces Together." *Communications Week*, Oct. 14, 1996.

Interview with Charles Wang, April 2000.

Moltzen, Edward F. "Software Management Mogul—Charles Wang." *Computer Reseller News*, Nov. 15, 1998.

Olsen, Florence. "Wang: Group Your Resources." *Government Computer News*, Mar. 3, 1997.

Pepe, Michele. "Charles Wang—with a Knack for Evolving, Wang Has Guided CA from the Age of Mainframes to Client/Server Computing." *Computer Reseller News*, Nov. 16, 1998.

Royal, Weld. "The Global Marketer." *Sales & Marketing Management*, May 1999.

Scher, Hager. "Wang's World." *Sky*.

Strugatch, Warren. "A Sensitive, Likable, Humble Guy (Who Knew?)." *LI Business News*, Oct. 22, 1999.

Teitlebaum, Richard. "Tough Guys Finish First." *Fortune*, July 21, 1998.

Tiazkun, Scott. "CA's Wang Weighs In on Global Issues." *Computer Reseller News*, Nov. 16, 1998.

Wintrob, Susanne. "CA's Wang Pleads Case for Legent." *Computer Dealer News*, Aug. 9, 1995.

Wang, Charles. *Techno Vision II*. New York: McGraw-Hill, 1997.

"Wang, Don't Outsource Business Mission." *PC Week*, Dec. 7, 1998.

"What We Can Learn from the Man Who Built the Second-Largest Computer Software Company in the World." *Boardroom*, Feb. 1, 1995.

# CHAPTER SEVEN

# SUMNER REDSTONE
## Chairman and CEO
### VIACOM/CBS

# The One Tough Cookie
# School of Mergers

*In 1979 Sumner Redstone was staying at the Boston Copely Plaza when the hotel went up in flames. The only way out of his room was via his third-story window. The fire burned about 40 percent of his body as he stubbornly and desperately held onto the ledge with one hand, awaiting help. It was a sobering lesson in "staying the course, hanging in there, refusing to drop—having the confidence [that] I could make it."*

—SUMNER REDSTONE

It has all the ingredients of a TV movie of the week. The hero is caught in a conflagration. There is no escape. He clings tenuously to a ledge 30 feet above the ground, the flames licking at his body. Finally, after what seems like hours, but is more likely just moments, he's rescued. His body is burned, but he lives—and survives, the experience a spur to go on and accomplish great things.

Sure, it's hokey. But it actually happened to Sumner Redstone, a kind of truth-is-stranger-than fiction, life-altering experience.

In 1979 Redstone was staying at the Boston Copely Plaza when the hotel went up in flames. The only way out of his room was via his third-story window. The fire burned about 40 percent of his body as he stubbornly and desperately held onto the ledge with one hand, awaiting help.

"When I got out of the fire, I couldn't lift a paper," he told *Financial World* magazine in 1994. "The pain was beyond belief. In those days, they didn't have artificial skin. They had to take the skin off the rest of your body. It was a horror."

But when Redstone survived, he seemed almost inspired by the near tragedy. It was, he's said, a sobering lesson in "staying the course, hanging in there, refusing to drop—having the confidence [that] I could make it." He was 56 years old when he was trapped by the flames. But he seemed like a 20-year-old when he survived, attacking life and the business world with a zest, vigor, and purpose he had never demonstrated previously.

"I think I was always driven before," he said. "But out of that fire came most of the exciting things I have done."

Redstone believes that "great successes are built on taking the negatives in your life and turning them around—taking a negative and turning it into a positive, overcoming hazard, overcoming danger, [and] overcoming catastrophe."

In many ways, Sumner Redstone's story is classic Horatio Alger. He was born in 1923 in Boston, the son of parents who had emigrated from Germany. He spent much of his early years living in a tenement with a bathroom down the hall. His father started with nothing, sold linoleum out of the back of a truck, and eventually owned two nightclubs (including the Boston Latin Quarter, which he purchased from Lou Walters, Barbara Walters's dad). He then opened one of the country's first drive-in movie theaters, on Long Island, the basis for what was to become the Redstone empire.

Sumner prospered as a child, prodded by parents who always wanted him to do more. "My mother was very tough," Redstone recalled in a 1999 interview. "When I used to practice piano for an hour, she would turn the clock back when I wasn't looking." Redstone responded well to his parents' entreaties. He was an exceptional student, gaining admittance to the prestigious Boston

Latin High School, one of the most difficult secondary schools in the country to get into and one of the most difficult to stay in. Half the typical freshman class does not make it to graduation. Not only did Redstone graduate; he finished first in his class and won every major academic honor.

By comparison, he's said, Harvard—which Redstone entered at age 17 with the class of 1944—was like kindergarten, and he breezed through there in just two-and-a-half years. A professor drafted him to join an elite Army intelligence unit that was credited with breaking several important Japanese codes. When the war was over, he returned to Cambridge and attended Harvard Law School.

---

# IT WAS AS THOUGH HE HAD A CRYSTAL BALL

Redstone worked in law for seven years after graduation, first as a law secretary to the U.S. Court of Appeals, then as a special assistant to the U.S. attorney general, and finally as a partner in a prestigious D.C. law firm. In 1954 he opted to return to the family business, a Dedham, Massachusetts-based chain of 12 drive-ins now called National Amusements. He immediately set about revitalizing the company, adding screens and getting better films to put on them. Even at this early stage in what would become a lengthy business career, Redstone started to demonstrate traits that would stand him in good stead during his years of M&A.

For one thing, it was almost as though he could look into the future. "Visionary" is a much overutilized word, but it did appear that Redstone had his own crystal ball, some kind of private pipeline to the months and years ahead. Consider that Redstone eschewed the conventional wisdom of that era, when most new movie theaters were being built in leased mall space. Instead, he made his cinemas freestanding and put them on land the company owned. As the value of the land soared, it ultimately increased the asset value of National Amusements—and played an important role in Redstone's ability to pull off his first acquisition.

Now consider another sign of Redstone's vision: As his father put up the third drive-in theater in the United States, Sumner became one of the originators of the multiplex concept.

But Sumner was more than just a corporate soothsayer. From the start, too, he demonstrated confidence in himself and his abilities to manage the company. He wasn't officially the president of National Amusements when he returned, but he took charge right away; he did not receive the title until 1967. "Optimism can be a driving force for a company," he's said. "And what is optimism? Confidence in your ability."

Another key Redstone characteristic is a competitive streak that makes even the *possibility* of losing unthinkable. "Well, anybody who is content to be less than first can't be number one." Redstone has said. "So you'd better want to be number one, it seems to me, more than anything. If you want to win, you have to want to win."

It is, by his own admission, that competitive spirit that drives him. "It's certainly not connected to the acquisition of money," he's said. He's not interested in many of the so-called rewards money can buy. Until recently, he still lived in the same home he originally bought in 1950. He used to send aides out to buy him batches of suits from Filene's.

"I'm not saying that money is not important. I think people who are really driven to succeed are driven by other things...whatever I've done, good or bad in my life, there's been an obsessive drive to win, to do it the best."

Fueled by that competitive drive, he has time and again shown a willingness and ability to fight for what he wants. Fittingly for the man who went on to acquire the CBS television network, he has consistently echoed the words of screenwriter Paddy Chayefsky (mouthed by Peter Finch) in the motion picture *Network*: "I'm mad as hell and I'm not going to take it anymore."

When he came back to National Amusements, for example, he took on the film studios in court, demanding that they extend to his little 12-drive-in chain the same rights for first-run films as they do to the big boys.

"We had to be combative, " he's said. "These companies were predators and didn't want us to get first-run products." He won. And over the course of the next couple of decades, he aggressively increased the number of National Amusements screens—to 50, 100, 200, and more.

It was a complete and, presumably, satisfying career. In all likelihood, Redstone would have retired as head of National Amusements, turned the privately held company over to his kids, and gone off on a long vacation— or at least as long a vacation and retirement as he is capable of.

Then came the fire.

And the equation changed.

"It seemed like forever," he said about the time he spent hanging from the ledge. A gruesome reminder of that day is always with him: his mangled right hand, missing its tendons, it's pinky cut off at the first joint. In the immediate aftermath: he went through "a very, very tough time." He seemed depressed, a feeling that lingered for several years.

Not surprisingly, he reexamined his life and, like the singer Peggy Lee, asked himself, "Is this all there is?" He'd built the family company way beyond anyone's fondest expectations, going from a dozen to several hundred screens. He was wealthy. But so what?

At around that time he was quoted as saying, "I have a big sense that it doesn't make much difference to the world whether we have 300 theaters or 400 or 500." He longed to do something "meaningful."

At the same time, nervous that the theater industry had peaked, he was growing increasingly concerned about the future of his business. Starting in the early 1980s, he began to invest in other, almost always related companies: Columbia Pictures and Loews Corporation, for example. He once attended a screening of *Star Wars* and was so impressed with George Lucas's film that he went out and purchased 25,000 shares of 20th Century Fox, the company that produced it.

In 1985 he bought a minority interest in Viacom, never intending it to be more than an investment, in the same way he had invested in other media companies. At about the same time, Carl Icahn made a bid for Viacom and was ultimately bought off with an expensive and extensive greenmail.

Then, inexplicably to Redstone, Viacom management made a buyout offer that seemed low and that included a business plan which would require the breakup of a company Sumner had grown fond of.

# NOT A GOOD MAN TO UNDERESTIMATE

At the time, Redstone said, "We were left with a choice: go away or take on the battle." If he'd walked away, he would have done so with a significant profit. But he had long come to the conclusion, based on his experience in the motion picture industry, that it was the product—what he came to call the software—not the distribution system, that made the difference. He had learned that the fanciest theaters would sit empty if there wasn't a good film playing. This notion seems largely elementary right now, but at the time it was not the prevailing view. Unlike Redstone, most people in the mid-1980s didn't yet see fractured network television audiences and declining Nielsen ratings in their futures.

So Redstone began to acquire stock. No one—least of all Viacom's management—paid attention to him. They considered him a two-bit theater owner from Boston and became the first of many groups to underestimate him.

# WILLING TO FIGHT FOR WHAT HE WANTS

It was a fierce battle between Redstone and the management group, with both raising their offers and counteroffers. Redstone felt, perhaps correctly, that the management was being tipped off about his offers by members of the board. At one point he exchanged nasty words with Viacom's chairman, and ultimately he even threatened to sue if his offer did not receive a fair hearing.

Redstone believes that if you are right, you will ultimately prevail. And ultimately he did. An investment banker who advised the management group later admitted that his side made one key error: It underestimated just how tenacious Redstone could be.

He officially landed Viacom in June 1987 for $3.4 billion. Again, he demonstrated several traits that were characteristic of his M.O. Coveting control, he resisted the idea of bringing in partners to help finance the Viacom deal (and assume part of its risks). Because he'd spent so many years as "The Boss" at National Amusements, it would be difficult to suddenly share power.

Still, he knows his strengths and weaknesses. Viacom was a highly diversified company in, as he put it, "so many different, but related, businesses, all of which I view as being on the cutting edge of excitement and growth and really of the whole technological revolution."

It was an area that was new to him. He admits that when he first began to purchase Viacom shares, "I knew nothing about cable—nothing about music networks or programming either. But I went around asking questions until I got answers."

To his credit, he recognized the need to bring in an expert in the field who could run the company and teach him the subtleties of the business. That man was Frank Biondi, a Coca-Cola executive who had been one of the key people in the early days of HBO. (Interestingly, there was some speculation that the reason Biondi was fired eight years later was because he'd taught Redstone all he could and was therefore expendable.)

Redstone soaked up the new knowledge: "One of the things I've learned that Frank had to teach me is that in my business—in my original business—you have a motion picture, you have an audience in the consumer—nobody stands in the way. They can walk into the theater and see the picture. Now [in cable television], theoretically, you can have the best pictures in the world, you can advertise them to the consumer, and they still have to walk their way through whatever packaging or whatever else the cable operator is doing before it happens."

# WILLING TO FIGHT FOR WHAT HE WANTS (PART II)

Redstone's inability to get his newly acquired Showtime network on more cable systems was particularly vexing. Ultimately, he sued HBO, charging that payments the company made to cable operators unfairly limited Showtime promotional opportunities. He went ahead with the suit even though he recognized he'd be getting the same cable operators he needed on his side very, very angry.

"We incurred the wrath of the cable industry at the time because the cable industry felt that they would be exposed in the process, [as would] a variety of anticompetitive practices that in fact existed." Still, Redstone weighed his options and went ahead with the suit. "The survival and success of Showtime was far more important than the downside that there was to filing the lawsuit," he said. Ultimately, Viacom and HBO reached a settlement.

Another trait he's shown consistently throughout his career is an ability to be adaptable. He's not locked into a single game plan and will willingly and quickly change direction as conditions demand. Consider that the Viacom purchase left him with substantial debt, $2.2 billion worth. Interest payments on that debt *for the first six months of 1988* were $188 million.

The logical course would have been for Redstone to sell off assets. And, in fact, an agreement he'd made with one of the lending institutions that backed him specified that he'd get rid of MTV within two years of the buyout. But as he got increasingly involved with Viacom's various assets, he saw a tremendous potential for the network. "I didn't like the music," he said at the time. But a year later, he added, "I still don't like the music, but I've become enamored of the economics."

Today, MTV and its various derivative networks (including VH-1) are in over 300 million homes around the world, and the network is one of the company's most profitable divisions. "Getting out of that agreement was something we had to do."

Similarly, Redstone has demonstrated again and again a willingness to forgo short-term profits to build value over the long term. Despite the heavy debt burden he faced early on, he continued to invest in Showtime. More recently, he invested $400 million in an animation studio for Nickelodeon, and to date, he has thrown hundreds of millions of dollars into the (up to now) hapless UPN network he acquired with Paramount Pictures.

The acquisition of Paramount in 1993, like his related purchase of Blockbuster video stores, was a vintage Redstone deal. He and Paramount Communications chief Martin Davis put together a friendly $8.2 billion deal to unite the two companies. In fact, Redstone believed it a done deal—and was already bragging about its potential—when a surprise $9.5 billion bid by long-time media executive Barry Diller threw a monkey wrench into the plans, setting off a bidding war.

Redstone got his prize, but paid more for it than he had intended. "We paid $10 billion," he said. "That's $2 billion more than we intended, thanks, as I like to say, to my $2 billion friend, Barry Diller." Interestingly, the two patched up any strains the Paramount battle might have caused in their long-standing friendship. "It's a mistake, if you want to run your company right, to let history get in the way of the future," Redstone contends.

The extra purchase price necessitated a deal with Blockbuster (more on that later), which provided the needed cash flow to pay off the massive debt Viacom had to take on.

Once again, the Paramount deal revealed aspects of Redstone's business personality that have contributed to his success. That competitiveness and bulldog determination—a stubborn streak, perhaps—all contributed to his success in the deal. He wasn't going to allow Diller to capture his prize.

A number of Viacom executives were very much opposed to the deal, convinced that the heavy debt incurred would force cutbacks in, and ultimately hurt, their operations. Redstone listened to what they had to say, but, as always, followed his own muse. "The opportunities we will have if we own Paramount will dwarf the opportunities at Viacom," he said during the negotiations. "Somebody has to make those decisions."

The merging of cultures and people was easy, as Redstone saw it: "Everyone is going to play an important role. The exact roles are not known yet....[My] point of view is simple: We don't care who came from where. The question is what particular piece of management has the best skills to handle all the assets. I'm not so much interested in who will take over what as in how you integrate two companies."

---

## COST IS LESS IMPORTANT THAN POTENTIAL

While Redstone certainly paid more for the two companies than he would have liked, he didn't foresee that as much of a problem. Like all the great M&A executives, he was less concerned with the purchase price than with the value added. "What people are missing when they are talking about the price being too high or too low—the real consideration isn't the dollars," he claims. "The real consideration is the combination."

He strongly believed that the whole was greater than the sum of its parts. "What is exciting to me is the exploitation of the really extraordinary powers of the combined franchise—power we can provide programmers in the middle of this global and technological revolution. Paramount is a programmer. We are a programmer with a proliferation of opportunities.

"I've had competitors say to me [that] we are going to be the single most powerful entertainment and communications company in the world. Think about this: You have MTV in [300] million households, growing fast in South America, and so on—Nickelodeon, Nick at Nite, VH-1, Showtime, The Movie Channel, Flix...that's an array.

"I think [that] in that area we may be dominant; we are certainly one of the dominant programmers. Take that together with the Paramount library—think of all the uses you can put that software to."

Everywhere Redstone looked he seemed to find synergistic opportunities. In a speech to the Washington Press Club late in 1994 he said, "For Viacom, the vision has always been consistent and clear: Mainly, the exploitation of our copyrights in every window provided by every technology and the control of software—by which I mean not just movies and television programming, but books, magazines, toys, games, video games, and merchandise—would be the key to success, regardless of the superhighway....

"Viacom will remain a software-driven company with a mission to drive that software through every distribution system to every multimedia application and to every region of the world."

# KEY INGREDIENTS TO SUCCESS: SYNERGY AND OPTIMISM

Viacom's executives were forbidden from putting their own division's interests ahead of the company's as a whole. Redstone forced Paramount Pictures to make movies developed by MTV and Nickelodeon—though executives from both sides resisted at first. In the end, however, Redstone was right more often than he was wrong, a case in point being *The Rugrat Movie*, made for $25 million and grossing about four times that.

Another facet of his personality is his constant and consistent optimism. Asked once what would happen if the spurting growth of the cable industry stalled, he called it a "possibility I refuse to acknowledge. It seems to me [that] the forces at play that are enhancing the

growth of cable and enhancing the growth of these channels don't seem to be abating. There is an erosion of the
major broadcast networks, and they do try to meet that
by increasing their prices in order to maintain their
income. All that works in favor of cable."

He also proved how good a negotiator he was. After
taking control of Paramount, he sold Madison Square
Garden (for over $1 billion), the educational publishing
division of Simon & Schuster (for $4.6 billion), and
other assets (for about $7.5 billion), far more than any-
one had expected. Not only did he slash Viacom debt
from about $11 billion to $4 billion, but he retained
about $4 billion in assets. Since he paid only about $10.2
billion for the whole kit and caboodle—after a bidding
war—he made a nice, quick profit for the company in
the blink of an accountant's eye.

If he's had a misstep, it was with his purchase of
Blockbuster. There was a widespread feeling within the
financial community that Blockbuster's videos were old
technology and "so very five minutes ago," as the current phrase goes. The executive Redstone brought in to
run the company didn't improve matters. The operation
was a mess, literally and figuratively.

"I walked through about seven warehouses of unbe-
lievable retail merchandise," Redstone recalls. "Hats,
T-shirts, cookies—they [even] had a bubble-gum pop-
gun. The stores were cluttered with all kinds of junk.
I found everything but ladies' underwear. Moreover,
when customers came in to rent tapes, there was a good
chance that the tape they wanted wasn't in stock."

The financial community became convinced he'd lost
his touch. "Everybody treated me as if I was stupid," he
remembers. "Nothing I'd done before mattered."

It was not the first time people underestimated him. The old Viacom management thought he was an old fogy. During the battle for Paramount, the prevailing wisdom was that Diller was the genius and would prevail. Even after Redstone won the battle, some were convinced he'd paid too much. And when he fired Frank Biondi, the word was that Redstone was too old and too out of touch to run a modern media giant. ("What has age got to do with vision, achievement, activity?" he wonders.)

In each case, the naysayers were proven wrong time and again, and the situation with Blockbuster would be no exception. At the time, typically Blockbuster paid the film studios about $65 a tape. So it was a financial hardship to order more than two or three of even the biggest blockbusters (with a small "b") for every store. This meant that many customers walked away from the store disappointed—and without a tape. Research indicated that so many people were disappointed so often, that they stopped trying to rent.

Redstone reasoned that video stores weren't all that different from the movie theaters he used to run. Both were channels of distribution of movies from the studios to the consumer. Studios didn't charge theaters a flat-fee up front, so why should they charge video stores one? He came up with an idea and personally got involved in selling it to the studios. They didn't like the idea at first, but Redstone's persistence and enthusiasm turned the day. He just focused on the problem, created a solution, and wouldn't give up until he'd sold it.

Currently, a typical deal works this way: Blockbuster pays about $7 for a tape, meaning it can get about nine times as many tapes as before for the same dollar. It gives the studio 40 percent of gross revenue for the first six months of the tape's release and smaller and smaller amounts after that. And when rentals of that particular film taper off, Blockbuster sells excess used copies for about what it paid for them new originally.

Who knows whether Redstone will ever stop buying companies. But for the moment, the cherry on his cake is his $35 billion merger with CBS. After all, he's said, "Viacom is me. I'm Viacom. The marriage is eternal— forever." In some ways, the CBS merger is a typical deal, in that it makes an already big company bigger: The combination of Viacom and CBS creates the third largest media company after Time Warner and Disney.

The merger also creates great synergy in terms of marketing and sales. Redstone has created a one-stop shopping center for advertising, whether the brands want to reach older folks (the CBS audience), younger adults (MTV and VH-1), or children (Nickelodeon). It's all there, and the cross-merchandising opportunities that will come out of it no doubt have the marketing department salivating.

But the deal is in some ways atypical of Redstone deals. For one thing, he's agreed to share power with CBS honcho Mel Karmazin, prompting the naysayers to be at it again: "It will never work. They won't get along." That all still has to be worked out, of course, but no one ever got rich betting against Sumner Redstone.

# REFERENCES

"Affiliates Wary of CBS–Viacom Deal." *Television Digest*, Sept. 13, 1999.

Bachman, Katy. "Moguls Urge Merger." *MediaWeek*, Nov. 1, 1999.

Beale, Claire. "Viacom and CBS Deal Creates Mega-brand Broadcast Giant." *Campaign*, Sept. 17, 1999.

"Blockbuster Improves Financials."*Supermarket News*, Nov. 8, 1999.

Bryant, Adam, with Brown, Corie. "The Making of a Media Giant." *Newsweek*, Sept. 20, 1999.

Gallese, Liz Roman "I Get Exhilarated by It." *Forbes*, Oct. 22, 1990.

Greenwald, John. "The Deal That Forced Diller to Fold." *Time*, Feb. 28, 1994.

Gubernick, Lisa. "Sumner Redstone Scores Again." *Forbes*, Oct 31, 1988.

Gunther, Marc, "Sumner [Heart] Mel." *Fortune*, Oct. 11, 1999.

_____. "Viacom: Redstone's Remarkable Ride to the Top." *Fortune*, Apr. 26, 1999.

Harris, Kathryn. "Can Redstone Really Take Back Seat at Viacom?" *Los Angeles Business Journal*, Nov. 15, 1999.

Haugsted, Linda. "Redstone: We Don't Need an AOL-y Ally." *Multichannel News*, Jan. 17, 2000.

Hearn, Ted. "Redstone Doesn't Fret over Powerful MSOs." *Multichannel News*, Apr. 17, 2000.

Higgins, John M. "Redstone and Biondi at Year Five." *Multichannel News*, June 1, 1992.

_____. "Redstone, Biondi Both Confident about TOPS." *Multichannel News*, Mar. 25, 1991.

_____. "Redstone Rift Booted Biondi." *Multichannel News*, Jan. 26, 1999.

_____. "Redstone's Inside Buys Puzzle Viacom Watchers." *Multichannel News*, Sept. 17, 1990.

Holstein, William J. "MTV, Meet 60 Minutes." *U.S. News & World Report*, Sept. 20, 1999.

"Indecent Proposals." *Economist*, Sept. 25, 1993.

Kadlec, Daniel J. "How Blockbuster Changed the Rules." *Time*, Aug. 3, 1998.

Kadlec, Daniel J. *Masters of the Universe*. New York: Harper Business, 1999.

Lenzner, Robert, and Matzer, Marla. "Late Bloomer." *Forbes*, Oct. 17, 1994.

Lenzner, Robert, and Newcomb, Peter. "The Vindication of Sumner Redstone." *Forbes*, Jan. 15, 1998.

Matzer, Marla, and Lenzner, Robert. "Winning Is the Only Thing." *Forbes*, Oct. 17, 1994.

McCarroll, Thomas. "A Blockbuster Deal for Beavis and Butt-Head." *Time*, Jan. 17, 1994.

McClellan, Steve, Higgins, John M., Trigoboff, Dan, and Schlosser, Joe. "The Mel-ding of Viacom, CBS." *Broadcast & Cable*, Sept. 13, 1999.

"Opening NAB Speakers Say TV Industry's Future Is Indeed Bright." *Communications Daily*, Apr. 11, 2000.

Picker, Ida. "Sumner Redstone Tests His Luck." *Institutional Investor*, Nov. 1995.

"Redstone Says Viacom–Paramount Deal Could Just Be the Beginning." *Communications Daily*, Sept. 14, 1993.

Schifrin, Matthew. "I Can't Even Remember the Old Star's Name." *Forbes*, Mar. 16, 1992.

Siklos, Richard. "They Have It All Now." *Business Week*, Sept. 20, 1999.

"Starting Over at Viacom." *Broadcasting*, Nov. 23, 1987.

Stern, Christopher, "Ready to Take On the World," *Broadcasting & Cable*, Sept. 20, 1993.

"Sumner Redstone: A Drive to Win." *Broadcasting*, Nov. 14, 1988.

Sweeting, Paul. "Not So Fast, Sumner." *Video Business*, June 29, 1998.

Traub, Stephen "Redstone in Motion: Here Comes Viacom, the World's Most Interesting Entertainment Company. And the Trickiest to Invest In." *Financial World*, Dec. 6, 1994

Troy, Mike "Power Players Make Power Moves." *Discount Store News*, May 5, 1997.

Zoglin, Richard. "A Firing at Fort Sumner." *Time*, Jan. 29, 1996.

# CHAPTER EIGHT

# STEVE CASE

Chairman and CEO

## AMERICA ONLINE

## Building a Business on the Premise that Technology Should Be Accessible

*The geeks didn't like us. They want as much technology as possible, while AOL's entire objective is to simplify. There is an inside Silicon Valley syndrome that is out of touch with what the consumers want. Our market is everybody else....*
*Right now, there's too much focus on technology and not enough on the consumer....We have a real obsession on consumers and what they want and how they want it. We can't get too caught up in the latest press release, the latest technology, the latest this, the latest that. We must focus on what the consumers want and [on] trying to stay really close to them.*

—STEVE CASE

Some time in the early 1980s, Steve Case plugged a telephone into his Kaypro computer and tried to go on-line. The on-line world has changed so much since then that it's difficult to remember what it was like back then, when just plugging a modem into a computer and dialing out was a high-tech adventure. This was before most people could even imagine a life that included e-mail and chat rooms and the ability to hook up a computer to the universe.

It cost Case literally thousands of dollars for the modem, the computer, and appropriate software. But even after he made the investment, it was nearly impossible to hook up to anything. And once he did hook up, there was no "there" there—no graphics, no color—just little white letters on a green screen scrolling down at a maddeningly slow pace.

That *anyone* could make the leap from what was on that tiny Kaypro screen to the future seems unlikely. However, that is exactly what Case did. "Despite how hard it was to set up and use," he said, "something magical was happening. The ability to sit at your desk and access information and connect with people all over the world—how could that not, over time, be a huge business?"

This anecdote about the company, which has been told and retold in countless books and magazine articles, is extremely instructive about Case and what he brings to the table: prescience. For if Case can lay claim to anything, it is his clear vision of the future. Time and time again, he ignored scoffers and plunged ahead in directions conventional wisdom suggested would lead to ruin. He did it because he somehow seemed to know what lay ahead.

In the mid-1990s, he predicted that by the year 2005 AOL would be as big a force on the Internet as Microsoft was in software. Everyone laughed. The big shots with big bankrolls—Gerald Levin at Time Warner and John Malone at Tele-Communications, Inc.—had tried to play the interactive game and failed. Moreover, Microsoft was going to enter the field and take over, in the same way it has dominated every field it entered.

Bill Gates once told Case. "I can buy 20 percent of you. Or I can buy all of you. Or I can go into this business myself and bury you." The conventional wisdom was that Gates was right. In the "best Case" scenario, all he could hope for was to sell out while he could, take his profits, and go back to selling pizzas and packaged goods, fields he knew something about—before it was too late.

Case chose instead to stay true to his vision. Today, Tele-Communications, Inc., is part of AT&T, and unless there is some last-minute dramatic change, as you read this, AOL owns Time Warner. Case's prediction not only came true; it came true years earlier than even he dreamed possible.

But Case's keen future vision is only part of the reason for AOL's success. It is not only the future he sees, but the way he sees the future, filtered through the eyes of someone who doesn't pretend to be a technical wizard. He is an ordinary computer Joe and, in an almost Zen sense, he and most of his customers are one.

# IT'S ALL ABOUT THE TECHNOLOGY

Case has insisted that AOL focus on both its customers and their needs, a focus that defies the conventional wisdom, which, at least among the "digerati," was that the Internet service provider was ultimately doomed because it didn't have the latest technology. As Case said to *Time* magazine, "The geeks didn't like us. They want as much technology as possible, while AOL's entire objective is to simplify. There is an inside Silicon Valley syndrome that is out of touch with what the consumers want. Our market is everybody else."

In fact, at the core of AOL's success was the realization early on that the computer elite were outnumbered by the simple Case-like folk, interested less in how the computer works than in being able to click a button and have it work.

Case is no technological wizard. His wizardry is in another area: recognizing the potential of technology and then figuring out how to make it accessible to the masses. Besides, he contends, there are already enough people out there concentrating on technology. "Right now, there's too much focus on technology and not enough on the consumer."

Case has said repeatedly, "We have a real obsession on consumers and what they want and how they want it. We can't get too caught up in the latest press release, the latest technology, the latest this, the latest that. We must focus on what...consumers want and [on] trying to stay really close to them."

We need to "use technology to really enable and empower and drive this revolution, while recognizing that technology is really a piece of the puzzle, and not the puzzle itself."

Case's idea has never been to make AOL the most sophisticated Internet service provider on the block. On the contrary, from the beginning, the concept was to make it the simplest—the easiest to use. "Consumers don't care if they're on a TCP/IP data network or an .x.25 data network. They don't care if the content was created in HTML format or a Rainman format. They care about the experience."

Even today, Case thinks that AOL is too complicated. After AOL was simplified again and again, it peeves him that he needs thousands of people answering customers' questions, "explaining to them why something we think is simple is in fact something they think is too hard." It means that AOL is still not simple enough.

Case picked up his concern for customers early on in his life. He was raised in Hawaii, on Oahu, and with older brother Dan started a variety of businesses: selling lemonade from the lemons that grew in their backyard, selling seeds, and even hawking wristwatches. "From the beginning, it was clear I'd be an entrepreneur." He attended Williams College, where he started four businesses (including an airport shuttle service). After graduating, he joined corporate America, first at Pepsi and then at Procter & Gamble (P&G).

He learned a lot of marketing lessons at P&G, working on low-tech products that stood him in good stead

ever since. The most important lesson was that marketing can only go so far. If the product is no good, the best
marketers in the world can't sell it—more than once.
"Consumers are smart. Good marketing can only get you
a trial. If the product is bad, sales go over the cliff."

But he picked up something even more important
during his tour of duty at P&G, based in Cincinnati. He
was there when two early interactive players, Warner
Brothers and American Express, experimented in a kind
of primitive two-way television. It was called CUBE, and
all it really did was allow viewers to tell advertisers what
they did and didn't like on the tube. But it caught Case's
eye. He was enchanted with the possibilities.

From Cincinnati, he moved to Kansas City and went
to work for Pizza Hut, looking for new toppings. There
he learned another important law of business: if you
want to find out what the customer wants, you've got to
sit down with him or her, taste bud to taste bud, so to
speak.

It was around this time, in the early 1980s, that he
bought his Kaypro and modem, hooked it up to an early
Internet service provider called the Source, and, in a
clunky, very primitive way, found that he could "talk" to
people from around the globe.

---

# MAKING THE CONNECTION TO THE INTERNET—AND THE FUTURE

Understand that all this was before Windows 2000,
before Windows '98, before Windows 3.1—even before
MS-DOS was the operating système du jour. It was the
paleolithic age of computers, but Case made a connec-

tion between that and the AOL future, a connection he doesn't believe was all that remarkable.

"There was something magical about being able to sit home in Kansas City and talk to people all over the world. It wasn't a great leap of faith to think that if you made it affordable and easy to use, people would want it."

Case went from Pizza Hut to a Virginia company called Control Video, which was trying to market an idea a decade or so ahead of its time. It wanted to ship Atari video games over the telephone the way games are now commonly downloaded. But a month after Case got there, the company went belly up. So in 1985 he helped start Quantum, an on-line bulletin board for Commodore 64 users. By the middle of 1987, the company was already making a small profit, but the Commodore was losing its market share fast. It soon became clear that Quantum needed to be able to be linked to other computer platforms, too.

Over the next few years, the company did several things extremely well. It changed its name to America Online, resisted the temptation to merge with a larger company such as Microsoft, and stayed true to its vision of creating a simple, graphically attractive place for average users to visit.

And Case proved willing to spend money to make money. As early as 1993, he agreed to spend about $250,000—a more-than-considerable sum for the company at the time—for, as Kara Swisher puts it in *AOL.com,* "the carpet-bombing of America." Sample AOL disks went out, via direct mail, with music CDs, with boxes of breakfast cereal, and with magazines (from computer publications to an issue of *Reform Judaism*)—by the millions—indeed, by the *hundreds of millions*.

Although it is commonplace now, the idea of sending out software offering new members free time if they sign on was revolutionary back then—and potentially dangerous.

The old adage about being careful what you wish for proved true several times at AOL. At regular intervals, the company's promotions were so successful signing up new members, it couldn't handle the volume the newbies generated, earning AOL the sobriquet America On Hold.

Still, Case and his staff recognized that they had to take chances. It's competitors, such as CompuServe, had been around longer, and others, such as Prodigy (a joint venture of IBM and Sears), were better funded.

But going back to his P&G days, he recognized the limits of good marketing. At the same time he was signing up new customers, he was providing content—something for them to do when they got to AOL: Alliances were signed with Disney, Hachette Filipacchi, *The New York Times*, Time, NBC, and ABC. Their connection with AOL not only provided valuable content and visibility, but added a veneer of legitimacy to a company that many had never heard of. At the time, AOL was not a link to the Internet and the World Wide Web, but a place to visit on its own.

Until the end of 1994, all of AOL's spectacular growth was organic. But around that time, the face of the online community was beginning to change. Offering a self-contained community was no longer enough. AOL had to provide access to the Internet and the World Wide Web. Prodigy had announced that it would offer Internet access in the fall of that year, beating AOL to the punch. So speed was critical. AOL began acquiring companies, including BookLink Technologies (a browser) and Navi-

Soft (which sold publishing and development tools). Both were expensive purchases, but AOL was late to the party and had to pay a premium.

There were numerous other purchases in the next year: Advanced Network & Services, a networking company; Medior; Global Network Navigator; and WebCrawler, a search tool and an index to the Internet.

# THE ACQUISITIONS THAT DEFINED AOL

But two acquisitions—of CompuServe and Netscape—and its proposed merger with Time Warner are what ultimately have defined, and will continue to define, AOL. By 1996, H&R Block became disenchanted with its CompuServe subsidiary and tried to get rid of it. CompuServe reported a first-quarter loss that year of $29.6 million and then announced a $58 million shortfall in the second quarter. It had an awful lot of excuses for the loss. First there were the start-up costs of WOW!, a family version of its business-oriented service designed to compete with AOL, but that was too little, too late. Then CompuServe executives also blamed continued investment in infrastructure. But, ultimately, what was really hurting the company's bottom line and long-term outlook was CompuServe's inability to hang onto its members. Even though it signed up 900,000 new members in the second quarter, overall, its total number of subscribers declined.

Meanwhile, AOL was having problems of its own. In the summer of 1996, AOL went dark for 19 hours. It was finding it impossible to handle the increased usage that came after it went from billing subscribers by the hour (at $2.95) to a monthly fee ($19.95).

Case put a positive spin on events: "What was happening for really the first time was that we [were affecting] people's daily lives in a significant way. Suddenly, overnight, we became part of everyday life. That's why there was this national outrage and tremendous passion and frustration, because people needed us, and many of them loved us, and we had disappointed them." It was a coming of age for the medium.

Still, CompuServe held some appeal for Case. As Swisher noted in her book, with about 3 million members added to its own 8 million subscribers, AOL would become, without question, the dominant on-line service. It would be about five times larger than its nearest competitor, Microsoft Network (MSN). Buying CompuServe also meant that Microsoft, which was reportedly interested, too, couldn't. Finally, CompuServe's 80,000 or so modems would increase AOL's by 30 percent and ease or perhaps even eliminate the strain AOL's network was experiencing. (This "benefit" was to become less important as the negotiations proceeded.) Another potential plus for consummating the deal was that CompuServe was stronger than AOL in Europe and Asia and could help provide an entree for the AOL brand overseas.

While Case favored the deal, he had some reservations. AOL had enough on its plate without trying to absorb another troubled company. That would mean spreading its resources further, and it was not likely to be seen as a positive move on Wall Street. After all, if you can't manage your own house, why take in more boarders?

"We had been in a crisis mode at AOL, and so it felt a bit like it was not an ideal time. There was the risk of taking our eye off the ball and how that could be perceived."

The good news is that AOL did not allow itself to get caught up in the enthusiasm about the prospect of buying a former rival to push it into a bad deal. The bad news is that a better deal might just not happen. If it was going to work, it would require the cooperation of several companies, as well as a series of trades that more closely resemble NBA trades than those of corporate America.

Interest in CompuServe from the folks at AOL never entirely waned. If the deal, as originally conceived, didn't work, perhaps a modified version would. Instead of purchasing the whole shooting match—the on-line service and the network hardware that supported it—the idea became to just buy the former and get out of the networking business entirely.

---

# CONCENTRATING ON MARKETING ITS SERVICE MADE THE DIFFERENCE

Like CompuServe, AOL was—kind of—two operations in one: the on-line service and the networking or hardware part. Back in 1995, AOL had purchased its ANS Networking subsidiary for $35 million, but AOL was the subsidiary's only client! ANS never reached a strategic mass that made it big enough to compete for outside business. So it kind of just sat there, a minor, but persistent, drain on AOL resources.

The turning point came when AOL was able to secure a long-term networking contract with an ANS competitor that afforded it lower and controlled networking costs. That deal freed the company up to get out of the networking business altogether. Then everything fell into place.

In a complicated deal that involved WorldCom, H&R Block, Bertlesmann, and AOL, AOL wound up with CompuServe, its 2.6 million members, and an enhanced international presence. Moreover, by getting rid of ANS (at a significant profit) as part of the deal, AOL was able to concentrate its efforts on marketing its services and building content. The folks at AOL were jubilant and considered the deal, in Swisher's words, "the once unthinkable coup of the digital decade."

But there was more to come just a year later. When it occurred at the end of 1998, the acquisition of Netscape (for $4.2 billion in AOL stock) was called "the most momentous merger in Internet history" by *Time* magazine. As the publication noted further, "The initial spin...was that it put the world's leading on-line service first in line for electronic commerce and entertainment—a market that could be worth trillions in just a few years."

Netscape was the first truly modern Web browser. It was developed by Marc Andreesen and the team that had come up with the Mosaic browser. Netscape was a significant improvement over that early effort and really provided the jump start that made the World Wide Web accessible. Using Netscape, one found it suddenly *easy*—well, comparatively easy—to go from one site to another, to view graphics in all their brilliant hues, and to download to a Webhead's heart's content.

How good was Netscape compared to its limited competition? It had about 80 percent of the browser market in 1995. It charged for its product, but people were willing to pay.

Then Bill opened the flood Gates. Microsoft included its Internet Explorer free as part of its new Windows 95 operating system, and suddenly Netscape had the kind of competition from which it never really recovered. (In addition to Internet Explorer being free, Netscape was also hurt by the fact that Microsoft apparently failed to provide Windows code in a timely fashion to Netscape engineers. This delayed their ability to modify their browser for use with the new operating system.)

By the time it bought Netscape, AOL had long decided that Microsoft's Internet Explorer was going to be its Web browser of choice. With Explorer distributed as part of the Windows operating system in most of the world's computers, Case and AOL had few alternatives. "We will continue to bundle...Internet Explorer with AOL because we want to have AOL bundled with Windows," he said in an interview broadcast on CNNfn.

So if AOL didn't buy the browser, what did it fork over the $4 billion for? It bought Netscape's Web site, which was one of the most popular portals, or entryways, to the World Wide Web. The site was also a profitable on-line launching pad for a variety of entertainment and shopping sites. And Netscape came with a lot of additional on-line software. But AOL also bought the future, in the form of Netscape's programmers.

As one founder of a high-tech investment firm told *Time* magazine, "America Online [before Netscape] has built an exceptional franchise on a technology base that could charitably be called dated. It has been difficult for its partners to work with and for AOL itself to maintain."

He wasn't talking about the kinds of bells and whistles that technophiles adore: AOL, probably concentrating too much on its marketing efforts, wasn't keeping up with advances in basic technology. As the investment-firm founder noted, "Netscape gives Case both a battalion of geek programmers and the software they've been working on, from industrial strength Web tools to back office e-commerce programs." What most of these programs did was make it easier for customers to work their way around the net and to make purchases securely and in comfort.

The plan worked. It silenced the critics who had maintained that AOL was technologically behind the times. Now AOL clearly is the most dominant consumer Internet service.

But both the CompuServe and Netscape deals were dwarfed by what Case announced next. His acquisition of Time Warner created a Godzilla in a number of ways. Some of it goes back to that basic philosophy of Case's: Keep it simple. "People are demanding more," he told First Boston's Global Telecommunications Conference in the spring of 2000. "They are asking, 'Why can't my PC be as simple as the TV, and why can't my TV be as powerful and flexible as my PC?" The answer, apparently, is that AOL and Time Warner hadn't come together before, but their joint operation would benefit all of humanity.

"The fact is," Case continued, "convergence is changing consumers' expectations—and the more they get, the more they want. Frankly, it's something [Time Warner CEO] Jerry Levin has been talking about for years—and it's where the AOL–Time Warner story really starts. AOL Time Warner will lead the way in turning this vision into a reality—not only by providing all the separate pieces, but by connecting the dots for consumers in simple, convenient ways that improve their lives."

That's not surprising rhetoric coming from a business executive who wants the government to see the merits of a deal that unites two giants. But clearly, he has a point: There are few companies where, going in, the fit seems better, the synergies more obvious. Time Warner brings an immense dowry to the marriage: a name brand known throughout the world and a major film studio, record labels, magazines, a broadcast television network, and several cable networks.

In theory, AOL brings technological expertise and infrastructure. "We are poised to lead the next wave of growth," says Case. But the truth is that the future of the Internet isn't in digitized magazines or downloading music and films, although that will almost certainly be part of the next great wave. Rather, Time Warner brings two things far more important to the table. The most prosaic is a great cash flow: $27 billion in annual income and $6 billion in gross earnings, to pay for all the changes that will take place over the coming decade. But more important, Time Warner brings access to its 13 million cable households, where in all likelihood, the battle of twenty-first–century dominance will take place.

Even *Time* magazine recognized that it wasn't what AOL was after. No, Case "faced a future that may see Internet access become a commodity, and he lacked access to the leading source of broadband—the fat fast pipes of cable television that could carry vast amounts of Internet content."

Case recognized that what everyone is talking about won't happen on copper wires, clunking along at 56K modem speeds. No, it will zip along broadband wires that will include TV, local and long-distance telephone, the

Internet, of course, and perhaps even more services that are currently unimagined. As *Red Herring* noted, AOL's enemy isn't Microsoft any longer: "It's real long-term competitor [is] AT&T."

"Looking out over the next couple of years, we see a new world taking shape, where everything gets connected and transforms peoples' lives," Case told the First Boston CEO. "Just think about the four devices that now deliver a variety of services in the home: television, the PC, the stereo, and the telephone. Already the distinctions between these devices are blurring—and interactivity is connecting all of them."

While he awaits the approval of regulators, Case continues to look into the future. At a high-tech business conference at the end of 1999, shortly after the AOL–Time Warner deal was announced, he spoke via satellite:

"The first big challenge we face is sparking new innovation. Now, this one may seem obvious, but you'd be surprised at how many people think that all of the biggest developments have already happened and now we're doing just a little bit of fine-tuning and watching the profits roll in. Nothing could be further from the truth. The technology battle is far from over."

Then he spoke a little about the future he saw:

"Within three years, one billion people will be accessing the Web, many of them using new wireless devices. In other words, the Web will soon reach a vast majority of the world's consumers, and many of them will be online daily, everywhere they go. The competition for these customers will be intense."

But there's certainly no doubt who will be in the thick of the fray.

# REFERENCES

Albiniak, Paige "Promises, Promises." *Broadcasting & Cable*, Mar. 6, 2000.

"America Online's Case Open to Cable." *Multichannel News*, June 13, 1994.

Berniker, Mark. "Online with Steve Case." *Broadcast & Cable*, Oct. 24, 1994.

Case, Steve. Remarks at Israel 99 Business Conference, Dec. 13, 1999

———. Remarks on CNNfn, Nov. 24, 1998.

———. Speech at CS First Boston Global Telecommunications CEO Conference, Mar. 8, 2000.

———. Speech delivered to the Jupiter Communications Annual Conference, Mar. 5, 1998.

———. Speech delivered to the National Press Club, Mar. 5, 1996.

Gunther, Marc. "The Internet Is Mr. Case's Neighborhood." *Fortune*, Mar. 30, 1998.

———. "These Guys Want It All." *Fortune*, Feb. 7, 2000.

Koprowski, Gene. "AOL CEO Steve Case." *Forbes ASAP*, Oct. 7, 1996.

Krantz, Michael. "AOL, You've Got Netscape." *Time*, Dec. 7, 1998.

Loomis, Carol J. "AOL + TWX=???" *Fortune*, Feb. 7, 2000.

Nocera, Joseph. "The Men Who Would be King." *Fortune*, Feb. 7, 2000.

Okrent, Daniel. "AOL–Time Warner Merger: Happily Ever After." *Time*, Jan. 24, 2000.

Perkins, Anthony. "Why Steve Case Is a Genius." *Red Herring*, Mar. 2000.

Ramo, Joshua Cooper. "How AOL Lost the Battles but Won the War." *Time*, Sept. 27, 1997.

Swisher, Kara. "AOL.com: How Steve Case Beat Bill Gates, Nailed the Netheads, and Made Millions in the War for the Web." *The New York Times*, "Times Business," 1998.

Vogelstein, Fred "The Talented Mr. Case." *U.S. News & World Report*, Jan. 24, 2000.

# CHAPTER NINE

# C. MICHAEL ARMSTRONG

## Chairman and CEO

## AT&T

# Turning a Battleship on a Dime

*Here we are in this marvelous growth industry—the most fabulous growth industry for decades—and AT&T, the largest company in that industry, was not growing. It was defending a business that—on a stand-alone basis—was not even viable, given the technology and deregulation. We had to go on the offensive.*

—C. MICHAEL ARMSTRONG

When Michael Armstrong was brought in to run AT&T in 1997, the company was one sick puppy. Its condition wasn't terminal—yet—but if left untreated, AT&T could easily have gone the way of the companies that once made buggy whips and buckboards, fading not too gracefully into oblivion.

If AT&T was to avoid that fate, Armstrong would have to serve as both corporate executive and corporate paramedic, performing a business triage and initiating treatment quickly, before the situation deteriorated further.

As he recalled for *Money* magazine two years later, when he came aboard, "the strategy was to protect long distance, conserve capital, preserve cash flow, and be a strong earnings-per-share point-to-point company."

It was a sound sensible policy that AT&T had followed for years, becoming in the process one of the most widely held stocks in America, an old fashioned stick-with-it-until-you-retire secure security. Ma Bell would not let anyone down.

There was just one problem: AT&T was no longer functioning in Ma's—or Pa's—economy. The rules had changed. The playing field had shifted like Candlestick Park after a quake. And AT&T hadn't adapted.

"The problem is that we weren't growing", said Armstrong, "[yet] we were in the greatest growth industry in the world—telecommunications."

In fact, not only was AT&T not growing, but its market share in its core long-distance business was eroding. New players had entered the field, wilier, swifter, and more readily able and willing to adopt and adapt new technologies.

Not surprisingly, Armstrong found that the old gray Ma just ain't what she used to be. The company's long-distance market share had plummeted from about 80 percent in the early 1990s to only 60 percent at the close of the decade, a decline of 25 percent. What's more, with the threat of the Baby Bells entering the long-distance arena as well, some analysts feared that AT&T could lose another 20 percent of market share.

---

# BLOCKED FROM DIRECT ACCESS TO ITS CUSTOMERS

AT&T has another problem as well. Since the breakup in 1984, AT&T did not have direct access to its customers. The only way it could get to clients was through its former subsidiaries, the Baby Bells, who were charging the company an arm, a leg, and an ear—over $15 billion annually—to get into the homes of Mr. and Mrs. America, to use what the telecommunications industry calls "the last mile."

"If you have to go through your competitors," Armstrong asked rhetorically, "then how can you be effective in satisfying your customers?"

But long distance was only part of the problem. He also had to deal with the company's seeming inability to get into the local service market. The Baby Bells resisted opening up their markets to competition for local service, using primarily a variety of legal tactics to at least delay the implementation of the 1996 Telecommunications Act. So, in 1996 and 1997, AT&T attempted to enter the market by buying local service in bulk from Baby Bells and reselling it to the public. It turned out to be a less-than-inspired strategy that cost the company $4 billion in about two years of operation.

---

# A NIKE KIND OF GUY

Two years after the fact, Armstrong recalled the situation he faced for *Directors and Boards* magazine: "Here we are in this marvelous growth industry—the most fabulous growth industry for decades—and AT&T, the largest company in that industry, was not growing. It was defending a business that—on a stand-alone basis—was not even viable, given the technology and deregulation. We had to go on the offensive."

Fortunately, Armstrong is a Nike kind of executive. His philosophy seems to be "Just do it!"

His first step was to come up with a strategy. He spent his initial 90 days as chairman and CEO closeted with his executive troops, trying to figure out where the company was, where it ought to be, and how the executives were going to get there.

"I closed the top-management team in a conference room for three months," he said. "That's a long time. But during that time, we did something extraordinary: We hammered out a complete redefinition of our strategy for AT&T."

The strategy was simple. The new AT&T was going to finally jump aboard the broadband wagon and push, scratch, and pull its way to the conductor's position up front. Its new goal was not *just* to be America's long-distance company or America's wireless company, but to reach out and touch every American in every way, through phone service, video, and high-speed data. Instead of relying on copper, AT&T was going to use the cable industry's wiring to get into American homes. And that essentially meant going into the cable business.

The idea is so simple and logical, it's a wonder that previous management didn't think of it. Not only does it solve one of AT&T's biggest obstacles—the cable line to a house is that vaunted "last mile"—but it provides all kinds of opportunities for a company with AT&T's muscle and brand awareness. Not only can modern broadband lines bring cable into the house, but there's enough room on those wires for long-distance service, the Internet, and local service, to boot. Suppose a company like AT&T told its cable customers, "You're paying us $50 a month for cable, but if you take long distance from us, we'll throw in local service for 5 bucks—and unlimited high-speed Internet for $15 more." The opportunities for AT&T are mind boggling, and the potential savings to consumers are awesome.

Still, it was, and remains, a risky strategy. Not only is what Armstrong did—and continues to do, since it is a work in progress—difficult (the equivalent of stopping an aircraft carrier on a dime and then turning it 180 degrees with kamikaze pilots all the time bearing down on the ship), but it requires a complete change in attitude, both inside and outside the company. That is, Armstrong's ideas would not only have to pass muster internally, but on Wall Street as well.

For years, AT&T has been dependable if nothing else. What Armstrong proposed was to make the company a high flyer. From staid and rock solid, it would become a player. AT&T's stock would—or at least, in Armstrong's view, should—no longer be measured exclusively on current earnings per share. Instead, it ought to be judged on its potential, in the way Internet and biotechnology stocks are measured.

The new AT&T was going to have to invest heavily in acquiring new companies and upgrading facilities. The payoff would be down the road, when improvements would be in place and, presumably, cash would come rolling in. Short-term earnings would suffer.

But this was just the kind of challenge that Armstrong seemed to revel in. As a Bear Stearns telecom analyst told *Fortune* magazine's Andrew Kupfer in the winter of 1998, "Mike Armstrong cannot be criticized for inaction."

---

## TREADING WATER CAN BE DANGEROUS TO A COMPANY'S HEALTH

In a follow-up story five months later, Kupfer quotes an anonymous executive saying it's "rare to see a CEO who so readily exposes himself to risk. His people call him 'scary' and a 'maniac.'"

This was not the first time that Armstrong had turned a company around—and it was certainly not the first time he had done it in the face of persistent skepticism. In the early 1980s, he was head of IBM's efforts to introduce a new device called the personal computer. At the time, people were convinced that the PC was a product of IBM's arrogance. No one would buy those crazy machines.

In the early 1990s, he took over management of Hughes Electronics, whose profitable missile business was beginning to implode because of the end of the Cold War. Most observers were convinced that the company would fade away like others that relied primarily on military contracts. But he fooled them.

It was at Hughes that Armstrong first practiced steering aircraft carriers into sharp turns. He slashed costs by 30 percent, sold the company's auto parts and missile divisions, and concentrated on the company's expertise in the satellite business to build the extremely successful DirecTV business. It was a significant all-or-nothing gamble: that $200 million satellites that took four years to build would be shot miles into the sky and then work. They did—and so did his plan.

Now he would have to do it again. "I'm going through the toughest time, just [as] I did in '83 and '84 with the personal computer. The same tough time that we went through in 1992 and '93, with the commercialization of the space strategy. [But] this is more visible. I've never enjoyed so many critics and authors and helpers from the outside [telling me] what I should have done and what I could do."

Armstrong has shown the ability to climb over—or run through—walls before, a skill he picked up at an early age. He was born and raised in Detroit in 1938, the son of a manufacturer's rep for suppliers to the automobile industry. His first wall was learning how to write properly.

A left-hander, he learned to write, but in the wrong direction. He told *Fortune* magazine, "I can remember my mother sitting with me at the dining room table, evening after evening, [making me practice writing and repeating] 'left to right, left to right.'"

He credits his mother with inculcating in him the discipline he still brings to all his endeavors. She sat with him every night, too, as he practiced classical piano, an hour a day almost every day for seven years, encouraging him to go on, assuring him that he could master first this piece and then that one.

# IF ALL ELSE FAILS, SELL POPCORN

"We all tend to rise to the expectations of the people we love," Armstrong recalled. "My mother's attitude was that if you want to do it, you can. That instills a tremendous confidence—combined with a good dose of fear of failure."

Overcoming the worst reviews from critics also is a long-held talent of his. Armstrong tells a story about his high school years that illustrates perfectly the genesis of the can-do attitude he has demonstrated continuously as a corporate executive. As a five-foot, six-inch prospect, he tried out for the freshman football team. But the coach, convinced that the undersized Armstrong would be hurt, didn't even allow him on the field.

"I was so mad [that] I bought a set of weights and started eating five meals a day," Armstrong said. Somehow he had faith that he would not turn into a five-foot, six-inch 400 pound mascot—and he was right. Not only did he put on weight and muscle, but he grew a half a foot, was named captain of the team in his senior year, and won an athletic scholarship to Miami (Ohio) University.

He got another critical review from the man who eventually became his father-in-law. According to a tale Armstrong's told many times, his future father-in-law refused his daughter permission to follow Armstrong to Miami University and predicted that Armstrong, would end up "selling popcorn in Tiger Stadium."

Armstrong proved his father-in-law wrong, just as he has consistently proven corporate naysayers wrong. That's not to say his career has been one long joyride. In 1983, working on a new generation of PCs for Big Blue, Armstrong selected a single supplier of disk drives. When that company couldn't deliver, it meant delays in introducing the new product, allowed competitors a crack through which they could sell their products, and ultimately contributed to IBM's loss of dominance in the personal computer market.

"I'll never again single-source a major component in my life," he told *Fortune* magazine, which called the mistake the darkest blot in his career.

Another lesson from his IBM days concerned Ross Perot. Neither Armstrong, individually, nor IBM, collectively, understood the significance of Ross Perot's departure from Big Blue to found EDS. By taking over IT centers for major companies, Perot placed himself between IBM and its customers.

When he joined AT&T, one of Armstrong's biggest fears was that history would repeat itself—that large multinational companies would need assistance managing their telecommunications functions would and turn to others to help manage their global networks. AT&T had been trying to establish network management as a significant business, and Armstrong immediately okayed further expansion plans. "I'm not going to wait and let the same thing happen on my watch," he said.

That was one of the reasons he was so quick off the starting block once he arrived at AT&T. Develop a coherent strategy and then quickly put major building blocks in place was his approach. As he did at Hughes, he started attacking costs.

In 1997 the telecommunications industry average for expenses to revenue was 22 percent. At AT&T it was 30 percent and obviously unacceptable. He removed $1.6 billion in overhead in the first 12 months of his tenure alone and quickly eliminated another half-billion over the next year. This was important for two reasons. First, it allowed Armstrong to buy time. The continuing decline in market share and profits of AT&T's core long-distance business and earnings per share would at least partially be offset by these substantial cost savings. That in turn would allow him to continue his turnaround strategy, which would also affect profits over the short term.

## PUT THE COMPANY ON A DIET—AND CONVINCE THE WORKERS TO LIKE IT

But, second, the cost savings also made AT&T more competitive. As the company's expense-to-revenue figures indicated, at over one-third above the industry average, AT&T was bloated. "Very few competitive businesses have sustainable success if they're not the low-cost producer. This company has no excuse not to be the low-cost producer and use cost as an advantage in the market."

Of course, Armstrong had to make sure that the people bought into the strategy. He spent a lot of time out in the field, too, talking to his employees about the new strategy and convincing them to come aboard. He spent time with customers, too, talking and, more importantly, listening. He's been known to sit down and field orders at customer service centers, hoping to discover why there are delays and mistakes in filling customer orders.

"You've got to lead by example. There are CEOs who get to love their offices. You've got to understand the competition. You've got to give the same speech too many times....I write an article every month for the company newspaper. I do videotapes. I do company broadcasts. Communicate, communicate, communicate! You cannot be a remote image. You've got to be touched, felt, heard, [and] believed."

But he also thought it important to let his executive staff know that there was a new sheriff in town. Some executives believe in leading by consensus. Armstrong is not one of them. Consensus is nice, especially if you have time, but he didn't have that luxury. "You'd better lead by intelligence, instinct, [and] judgment, and make decisions while there are still some risks in them, or you're not going to lead in your markets.

"That was one of the problems here. They had one-stop shopping. Any manager at any level could stop any good idea forever. We had to cut through that and make decisions."

At the strategy sessions, he said, roughly 90 percent of his new team bought into the strategy. "The other 10 percent were people who weren't used to this new pace of activity. They were used to taking months and months for analysis, homework, and review. To some degree, moving [that] quickly was a risk. But I felt strongly that this strategy was the only way AT&T could fulfill its potential."

And he was willing to put his reputation on the line. Armstrong is a fervent believer in responsibility and accountability. In a speech before the Council on Foreign Relations delivered at the end of 1995, while he was still chairman and CEO of Hughes Electronics, he suggested that a no-fault mentality had crept into American business:

"The ancient Romans had a tradition," he said. "Whenever one of their engineers constructed an arch, as the capstone was hoisted into place, the engineer assumed accountability for his work in the most profound way possible: He stood under the arch. If his construction was shoddy, he would be the first to know. With our market system, American management must stand under the arch."

That's where he put his executives, metaphorically anyway. Perks were taken away. Life in an executive wing that had been known as "Carpetland" was going to be less plush. Demanding that executives give up their chauffeurs was probably not a big "penalty," all things considered, but that wasn't the point. The point was that the old AT&T way of doing things was going to change.

There were no longer going to be group bonuses based on how the company as a whole did. Henceforth, bonuses would be offered on meeting individual goals. Armstrong intended to offer stockholders more details, more detailed disclosure, and, for the first time, breakout revenues of different business units.

"We're going to segment the company [so as] to be accountable and be measured," he said. In other words, his people were going to have to stand under the arch.

And when they weren't under the arch, they were going to have to be out in the field. He required his top 100 officers to own at least three major accounts—and call on them at least twice a year to get a sense of what was going on.

But the key to the strategy was AT&T's ability to acquire cable companies. Armstrong went on a buying spree. In his first year, he bought cable giant Tele-Communications, Inc. (TCI), Teleport Communications Group, a phone company that serves large corporations, and a couple of cellular phone companies. He formed a joint venture with British Telecom to combine international phone and Internet services. And he didn't stop at the end of the year.

The following year Armstrong continued his buying spree with IBM Global Network, which carries data traffic, and MediaOne, another cable operator. The latter deal made AT&T the largest cable operator in the land. It was, he said, "not just an investment in AT&T's future. It's an investment in the communications future of the entire country."

In short, what Armstrong has done is take a long-range view. Rather than try to beef up long-distance earnings artificially, he remained true to his strategy, even though that meant putting consumer long distance on a kind of life support.

Again, the logic of his thinking was impeccable. With the Baby Bells entering the long-distance markets, it seems inevitable that AT&T's share will continue to erode, no matter how many marketing and promotional dollars he throws at it. Still, even though its share is decreasing, long distance still generates billions of dollars in revenues that can be used to buy more cable companies or put in the broadband wiring in the companies AT&T already owns.

"It's a systematic, declining industry, long distance," he said. "That is irreversible—and not just for AT&T, but for the long-distance industry."

The good news for AT&T is that it is losing share in an area in which Armstrong and Co. have no control. And there seemed no point in wasting valuable people power and time fighting the inevitable.

The great news is that all the people power, time, and money devoted to the rest of the company seems to be paying off. If you take long distance from the mix, AT&T earnings were up in double digits for the first part of 2000, with prospects for those kinds of increases in the future. The figures are impressive.

Through its cable lines, AT&T said it would be delivering local telephone service to at least 400,000 subscribers by the end of 2000. Armstrong remains confident. At a press conference he explained why:

"I think that we're making some really sound progress. I think a lot of the progress is masked by financials as a result of the declining voice business.

"What gives me confidence to respond to that question [about confidence] rather than go look at the price of the stock and get depressed is that the investments and the strategy are working. I see it, and the people who take the time to look at our company know it."

Some others are beginning to notice. AT&T's joint venture with British Telecom is expected to go public in 2001, raising as much as $70 billion.

Will investors ultimately be as generous with AT&T shares? Will they when they realize that, although they thought they bought shares in what used to be known as American Telephone and Telegraph, they purchased Amazon-dot-com Telephone and Telegraph?

If not, Armstrong can always sell popcorn at Tiger Stadium.

\* \* \*

As this book was going to press, Armstrong demonstrated another facet of his character best summed up by county singer Kenny Rogers: "You gotta know when to hold'em; you gotta know when to fold'em." Though Armstrong's strategy made sense—and even appeared to be working—Wall Street didn't buy it. And the CEO realized there was no point in holding on to a bad hand.

So he announced that AT&T would split up once again, into four companies: wireless, cable, business service, and consumer telephone. He told analysts that his ambitious corporate efforts had been misunderstood and unappreciated. Also he was confident that with this new approach the "outcome would be successful."

# REFERENCES

Armstrong, Michael, Speech delivered at Telecom '99, Dec. 15, 1999.

_____ . Speech delivered before the Council on Foreign Relations, July 1, 1995.

_____ . Speech delivered before MICOM Advance Planning Briefing for Industry, Nov. 9, 1993.

_____ . Speech delivered to the Economics Club of Detroit, Sept. 29, 1998.

"AT&T Restructuring Ties Cuts to New Products, Compensation Attitude." *Communications Daily*, Jan. 28, 1998.

"AT&T Selects Hughes Chief Armstrong as CEO." *Communications Daily*, Oct. 21, 1997.

Creswell, Julie. "Telecom's Mixed Signals." *Fortune*, Apr. 3, 2000.

Donlon, J. P. "Now for the Hard Part." *Chief Executive*, Sept. 1999.

Goldblatt, Henry. "AT&T's Costly Game of Catch-Up." *Fortune*, July 20, 1998.

Greenfield, Karl Taro. "Ma Everything! With One Astonishing Deal, AT&T Hopes to Become a Communication Colossus—Again. This Is What It May Mean for You." *Time*, May 17, 1999.

Kupfer, Andrew. "AT&T Gets Lucky." *Fortune*, Nov. 9, 1998.

_____ . "AT&T Goes Cable Crazy," *Fortune*, May 24, 1999

_____ . "Mike Armstrong's AT&T: Will the Pieces Come Together." *Fortune*, April 16, 1999.

_____ . "Mothra and Godzilla Breed." *Fortune*, June 7, 1999.

Neff, Thomas J., and Citrin, James M. "Mike Armstrong's Principles of Leadership." *Director's & Boards*, Fall 1999.

Quint, Brian. "New Media: Stealing Home." *Telephony*, June 14, 1999.

Schaff, William. "The New (Improved) AT&T." *Information Week*, Feb. 8. 1999.

Schiesel, Seth. "With AT&T at the Brink, Pressures Rise at the Top." *The New York Times*, July 9, 2000.

Vogelstein, Fred. "AT&T + TCI=Telecom Muscle Galore." *U.S. News & World Report*, July 6, 1998.

_____ . "Ma Bell Is Morphing into the Cable Guy." *U.S. News & World Report*, May 10, 1999.

_____ . "The Man with the Right Connections." *U.S. News & World Report*, Aug. 10, 1998.

_____ . "Michael Armstrong Finds His Calling." *U.S. News & World Report*, May 17, 1999.

Woolley, Scott. "Mike Strikes Back." *Forbes*, Dec. 13, 1999.

Woolley, Suzanne. "AT&T: What Have They Done to Ma Bell? AT&T Is Still the Most Widely Held Stock in America. Should It Be?" *Money*, Aug. 1, 1999.

# INDEX

ABC, 134
Advanced Network & Services, 135
Aetna, 50
Agent Works, 96
Allied Signal, 80
America Online (AOL), 127,
    129–131, 133–142
American Express, 45–47, 132
AMP, 33
Andreesen, Marc, 138
AOL (*see* America Online)
Applied Data Research, 101
Armstrong, C. Michael, 145–159
    on being the low-cost pro-
        ducer, 154–158
    at Hughes Electronics, 151
    persistence of, 151–152
    on responding to criticism,
        152–153
    on rising to others' expecta-
        tions, 152
    and Ross Perot, 153
    on strategy for AT&T, 148–150
Artzt, Russell, 88, 93
AT&T, 145–150, 153–159
Avis Rent-A-Car, 55

Baker, George P., 77, 78, 80, 82, 83
BankAmerica, 47–48
Bear Stearns, 75
Berlind, Roger, 44
Bertlesmann, 138
Biondi, Frank, 115–116
Blockbuster, 121–123
Boeing, 13
BookLink Technologies, 134
Bosack, Leonard, 5–6
British Telecom, 158

CA (*see* Computer Associates)
Cabot Corporation, 21
Capex, 98–99

Case, Dan, 131
Case, Steve, 127–142
    on AOL's "crisis," 136–137
    on challenges of the future,
        142
    on convergence, 140–141
    on customer focus, 130–131
    early life/career of, 128–129,
        131–133
    and growth of AOL, 133–135
    on Internet Explorer, 139
    vision of, 129–130
Cash flow, 23, 71–72, 76
CBS, 123
Cerent Corp., 8–9
Chambers, John, 1–14
    and acquisition of Crescendo
        Communications, 13–14
    acquisitions policy under, 6–7
    early influences/career of,
        3–6
    growth of Cisco under, 2–3
    on learning from mistakes,
        9–10
    long-range perspective of,
        7–9
    and shared vision, 10–12
Chambers, Raymond G., 54–55
Chayefsky, Paddy, 112
Cigoux, Mimi, 9
Cisco, 2–3, 5–14
Citibank, 43
Citicorp, 50
Citigroup, 50
Cogan, Berlind, Weill & Levitt,
    41–43
Commercial Credit Corporation,
    48–50
Compaq, 12
CompuServe, 134–137, 140
Computer Associates (CA),
    88–89, 93–103

161

Control Data, 48
Control Video, 133
Convergence, 140–141
Core businesses, identifying,
    24–25
Crescendo Communications,
    13–14
Criticism, responding to, 152–153
CUBE, 132
Cullinet, 97–98, 101
Culture, corporate, 12, 27–28
Customer, focus on, 130–131

Digital Equipment Corporation,
    12
Diller, Barry, 118, 122
DirecTV, 151
Disney, 134
Due diligence, 58–59
Duracell, 81
Dynaco, 18

EDS, 102, 103
Ellison, Larry, 103
Employees:
    avoiding layoffs of, 8
    positive environment for,
        8–9, 100–102
Entrepreneurial skills, 31–35
Expectations of others, rising to,
    152

FB Trucking, 83
Fear, 84
Filipowski, Andrew, 103
Fireman's Fund, 45–46
Fred Meyer Inc., 79

Gates, Bill, 129, 139
Gaziano, Joseph, 18
Geneen, Harold, 20
Gerstner, Louis, 2
Gibson Greeting Cards, 55
Global Network Navigator, 135
Gordon, Bob, 101

Griffey, Ken, Jr., 2
Gromer, Juergen, 33–34

Hachette Filipacchi, 134
HBO, 115, 116
Hirsch, Leon, 29
Hostile takeovers, 28
H&R Block, 135, 138
Hughes Electronics, 151, 154, 156

IBM, 4–5, 153
IBM Global Network, 157
Icahn, Carl, 113
Immediate benefits, demand for,
    25–27
Internet Explorer, 139

J.P. Morgan Bank, 60–61

Karmazin, Mel, 123
Kemp, Jack, 64
Kidder, Robert, 81
Kohlberg Kravis Roberts (KKR),
    70–72, 76, 77, 79–84
Kozlowski, L. Dennis, 17–35
    on avoiding pressure, 22–24
    on core industries, 24–25
    on demand for immediate
        benefits, 25–27
    early life/career of, 18–21
    on entrepreneurial skills of
        top executives, 31–35
    on finding potential acquisi-
        tions, 27–31
    and Tyco model for M&As,
        21–22
Kraft, 81
Kravis, Henry R., 69–84
    background and early career
        of, 72–77
    on fear, 84
    fundamental M&A rules of,
        76–77
    on long-range perspective, 81
    at Madison Fund, 74–75
    on saying "no," 78

Kravis, Ray, 72
Kumar, Sanjay, 95
Kupfer, Andrew, 150

Layoffs, post-acquisition, 8
LBOs (*see* Leveraged buyouts)
Legent, 96
Lerner, Sandy, 5–6
Leveraged buyouts (LBOs),
    54–55, 72
Levin, Gerald (Jerry), 129, 140
Licensing agreements, 102–103
Loeb Rhoades Hornblower, 43
Long-range perspective(s):
    of Henry R. Kravis, 81
    of John Chambers, 7–9
    of Sumner Redstone, 117
Low-cost producer, becoming
    the, 154–158
Ludlow (plastics company), 29

Madison Fund, 74–75
Malone, John, 129
Management, 77
Medior, 135
Merkle, Ed, 78
Microsoft, 129
Microsoft Network, 136
Mistakes, learning from, 9–10,
    26–27, 41–42
Morgridge, John, 6, 13–14
Mosaic, 138
MTV, 117, 119, 123

National Amusements, 111, 112,
    115
NaviSoft, 134–135
NBC, 134
Netscape, 138–140
Newport News Shipbuilding, 102
New York Stock Exchange, 42
*The New York Times*, 134
Nickelodeon, 123
"No," saying, 30, 78

Ownership, 49

Paramount, 117–121
Perot, Ross, 153
P&G (*see* Procter & Gamble)
Pizza Hut, 132
Platinum Technologies Interna-
    tional, Inc., 103
Potential acquisitions, finding,
    27–31, 63–65
Pressure, avoiding, 22–24
Primerica, 50
Procter & Gamble (P&G), 131–132
Prodigy, 134

Ragi, Sanjay, 101
"Redcoat" method, 63
Redstone, Sumner, 107–123
    adaptability of, 116–117
    early life/career of, 109–113
    long-term perspective of, 117
    as negotiator, 121
    and Paramount, 117–121
    on "staying the course,"
        107–109
    and Viacom, 113–115, 120–123
Reed, John, 50
RJR Nabisco, 83
Roberts, George, 75, 84
Robinson, Doug, 101

Salomon Brothers, 50
SCM Corporation, 19–20
Securities and Exchange
    Commission, 41
Shared vision, 10–12
Shearson, 50
Shearson, Hamill (company), 43
Showtime, 116
Simon, J. Peter, 62
Simon, William E., Jr., 53–67
    as district attorney, 56–58
    early influences/career of,
        59–62
    on finding companies to
        purchase, 63–65

Simon, William E., Jr., (*Cont.*)
    guidelines used by, 65–67
    and leveraged buyouts, 54–55
    "redcoat" method, 63
    and William E. Simon &
        Sons, 55–56
Smith, George David, 77, 78, 80,
    82, 83
"Staying the course," 107–109
Stewart, James B., 83
Stock, restricted, 49
Stone, Hayden, 41
Swisher, Kara, 133

Tele-Communications, Inc.
    (TCI), 157
Telecommunications Act of
    1996, 148
Time Inc., 134
Time Warner, 129, 140
Travelers, 50
Tri-State Motor Transit, 74–75
Troubled companies, 42–43, 98
Tyco International, 18–19,
    21–22, 24–35

U.S. Surgical Corp., 29

VH-1, 117, 123
Viacom, 113–118, 120–123
Vision, 10–12, 43–44, 110–111,
    129–130

Wang, Charles, 87–104
    background/early career of,
        88–94
    and Capex, 98–99
    on creation of positive
        employee environment,
        100–102
    on licensing agreements,
        102–103
    on life, 104
    on opportunities, 98
    on reasons for acquisitions,
        94–97
Wang Labs, 5
Warner Brothers, 132
WebCrawler, 135
Weill, Sanford I., 37–50
    at American Express, 45–47
    and Commercial Credit,
        48–50
    early career of, 38–41
    on family, 47
    on risk and making mistakes,
        41–42
    and troubled companies,
        42–43
    vision of, 43–44
Welch, Jack, 2
Wilson Sporting Goods, 55
World Wide Web, 3
WorldCom, 138
WOW!, 135

# ABOUT THE AUTHOR

Curt Schleier is a contributing writer to *Investor's Business Daily,* a syndicated book critic, and a regular contributor to a number of other business and consumer publications.